Guide to Sea Angling
in North Wales & Merseyside
Second Edition 2007

By Phil Simpson

Photos by Phil Simpson
Illustrations by Garry Gannicliffe

About the author

Phil Simpson began angling at the age of 10, on family holidays catching small coalfish from the Battery Pier, Douglas in the Isle of Man. His formative years were spent fishing the Mersey in the winter for dabs and whiting and summer to the pursuit of bass over the Bank off Hoylake. His first car opened up the North Wales coast and for 30 years he has been a regular visitor, spending most of his spare time enjoying the area's rich and varied fishing. Phil alternates between boat and shore, a fact reflected in his two best catches, a 180lb (81kg) common skate taken out of Westport, Co Mayo and four small eyed ray weighing between 8lb and 10lb 8oz (3.6 to 4.8kg) taken in four casts at Hell's Mouth, North Wales. Phil has been a regular contributor to 'Anglers Mail' since the 1980's and has also written many articles for 'Improve Your Sea Fishing' and 'Sea Fishing' magazines.

First published 1999
Second Edition 2007
Published by

LAVER *publishing*
PO Box 7,
Liverpool L19 9EN
www.laverpublishing.com
©1999 & 2007
Designed & illustrated by
Garry Ganncliffe
Photographs ©1985-2007
Phil Simpson
& ©1999-2007
Garry Ganncliffe
0 904825 40 X

All the content of this book is protected by Copyright and may not be used or reproduced in whole or in part in any physical or electronic form including but not limited to photocopy, fax, web page, e-mail, presentation or display without permission from the publisher.

CONTENTS

- INTRODUCTION 4
- SAFETY ASHORE & AFLOAT 5
- WHAT'S THE CATCH? 8
- TACKLE & BAIT 10

TOP FEATURES FOR ALL SEA ANGLERS

TOP MARKS FOR SHORE ANGLING

1. Pwllheli 12
2. Hell's Mouth / Porth Neigwl 14
3. Uwchmynydd 16
4. Whistling Sands / Porthor 18
5. Pistyll 20
6. Dinas Dinlle 22
7. Caernarfon 24
8. The Swellies 26
9. Bangor Pier 28
10. Pwllfanogl, Anglesey 30
11. Ty Croes, Anglesey 32
12. Cable Bay / Porth Trecastell, Anglesey ... 34
13. Porth Dafarch, Holy Island 36
14. Holyhead Breakwater, Holy Island 38
15. Bull Bay, Anglesey 40
16. Llam Carw, Anglesey 42
17. Point Lynas, Anglesey 44
18. Whitebeach, Anglesey 46
19. Deganwy 48
20. Llandudno Pier 50
21. Llandudno North Shore 52
22. Tan Llan 54
23. Mostyn 56
24. Greenfield 58
25. Caldy, Wirral 60
26. King's Parade, Wirral 62
27. Perch Rock, New Brighton 64
28. Egremont, Wallasey 66
29. Woodside, Birkenhead 68
30. Bromborough 70
31. Otterspool, Liverpool 72
32. Alexandra Dock, Liverpool 74

- ABOUT BOAT ANGLING 76
  1. Trefor Slipway 77-79
  2. Menai Bridge Slipway 80-82
  3. Trearrdur Bay Slipway, Anglesey ... 83-85
  4. Traeth Bychan Slipway, Anglesey .. 86-88
  5. New Brighton Slipway 89-91

TOP MARKS FOR BOAT ANGLING

DIRECTORY 92-96

INTRODUCTION

Having run a tackle shop on the North Wales coast for twelve years, one of the questions I was most frequently asked was "Where can we go fishing and what will we catch?"

In this new edition of his Guide to Sea Angling in North Wales and Merseyside, Phil Simpson, has put together a comprehensive selection of tried and tested fishing marks, marks that have the potential to produce good and varied fishing. In preparing the information Phil has employed his extensive knowledge of the Welsh and Merseyside coastlines, local fishing conditions and the best baits to use.

What the book offers, as the title suggests, is a complete guide to improving your fishing around North Wales and the Mersey, whatever your level of expertise. So whether you're just starting out or you already have some sound experience under your belt, and whether you prefer fishing from beaches or from rocks, this guide tells you all you need to know to boost your success rate and get even more enjoyment out of your sport.

You'll wonder how you ever managed without it.

Mike Robinson, Llandudno.

BEAUFORT WIND SCALE

Force	Knots	MPH	Description	Sea State
0	<1	<1	Calm	Like a mirror.
1	1-3	1-3	Light Airs	Ripples without foam crests.
2	4-6	4-7	Light Breeze	Small wavelets.
3	7-10	8-12	Gentle Breeze	Larger wavelets, crests begin to break about. A few white horses.
4	11-16	13-18	Moderate Breeze	Small waves with more white horses.
5	17-21	19-24	Fresh Breeze	Moderate waves, longer and with many white horses. Possibly some spray.
6	22-27	25-31	Strong Breeze	Long waves begin to form white foam crests. Usually with some spray.
7	28-33	32-38	Near Gale	Sea heaps up. White foam begins to be blown in streaks
8	34-40	39-46	Gale	Moderately high waves of greater length with foam blown in well marked streaks
9	41-47	47-54	Strong Gale	High waves with dense foam. Crests begin to topple and roll over. Spray affects visibility.
10	48-55	55-63	Storm	Very high waves with long overhanging crests. Large areas of white foam. Tumbling of the sea becomes heavy and shocking. Visibility reduced.
11	56-63	64-73	Violent Storm	Exceptionally high waves, sea mostly covered in white foam. Poor visibility
12	64+	74+	Hurricane	Air filled with foam and spray. Sea completely white. Very poor visibility.

SAFETY ON THE SHORE

There are places where sea angling is an almost completely safe activity, but there are also places where anglers face a certain degree of risk from natural hazards, man made hazards and the human factor. Help make the sport safe and enjoyable for all.

Natural Hazards
Never underestimate the power of the Forces of Nature.

Weather
Check the weather, looking out particularly for wind speed and direction as this can affect the tides. An onshore wind can cause the tide to continue rising after the predicted high water point. Low pressure brings high winds, sometimes a danger on exposed marks.

Tides
Make sure you can retreat from your position. The usual danger is being cut off by the incoming tide. When fishing from rocks keep a good lookout on the sea around you. On beaches check you are not stranded on a sandbar where gullies might cut you off.

The Sea
A calm sea itself holds dangers and it can change quite suddenly when the tide turns. The undertow of the surf can sweep an unwary or tired angler off his feet.

"Freak waves" are more common than you might suppose. These are caused when the natural rhythms of the sea coincide. Wind can intensify the effect and in extreme cases they can knock an angler off rocks or capsize a boat. Such extremes are rare but be prepared for the occasional unusually large wave.

Cliffs
Muddy or steep and rocky cliff paths might be easy enough to descend early in the day but climbing back, after a long day's fishing, can be more difficult.

Fish & Shellfish
Marine life can also be dangerous as some fish such as conger, tope, ling and whiting have sharp teeth, or spines like bass, black bream and wrasse.

When preparing shellfish as bait, perhaps with wet hands, be careful of sharp claws and jagged edges on shells.

Man Made Hazards
Other people's mess.
Sewage
The North Wales coast is famously clean and now the Mersey is too. In 1999 it was voted "Most Improved River in the World".

> Sometimes algae can be mistaken for pollution. This is a large mass of microscopic plants which bloom and die to form a foul smelling creamy-brown foam. Often called "May Water", this is quite unpleasant but generally harmless.

Oil & Chemicals
Report any instances of pollution you find to the Environment Agency.
Most of the sea areas covered in this book are very clean and the fish are healthy. The exception is bottom feeding fish from the Mersey which should not be eaten.

Dangerous Objects
Drums of chemicals and old ammunition sometimes reach the shore and should be dealt with by experts. If you find a suspicious object approach it with caution. Look for identifying marks or labels but do not touch it if it is damaged or leaking. In cases of obvious danger clear the area and send for help.
The local authority is responsible for such finds and it is usually advisable to inform the police.

The Human Factor
We all have a part to play.
Don't carry on fishing when you are worn out. Being cold, wet, tired and hungry while sea fishing is dangerous. Take a good packed lunch and some high energy food such as chocolate or glucose sweets.
Also consider other anglers. When casting make sure the area is clear. Ensure all rig connections are sound to avoid "snap-off", when the tackle flies off during a cast.
Tidy as you go. Tackle left lying around can be damaged or cause an accident and litter left behind is bad for the image of angling.

Safety Equipment
Ready for anything?
Clothing
The most important equipment for personal safety is your clothing. Whether it is a top of the range flotation suit or a simple sun hat, it must be up to the job.
Flotation suits can be real life-savers for shore anglers as well as those on boats. These brightly coloured one or two piece suits are waterproof, thermally insulated and are highly recommended for fishing where there might be a danger of falling in.
Appropriate footwear is also very important. If you plan to fish from rocks consider a good pair of walking or even climbing boots.
You will also need protection on sunny days. A sun hat that covers the nape of the neck will help prevent sunstroke and sunscreen lotion will protect against burning.

Equipment
Make sure you carry a watch and keep an eye on the time. Pack a first aid kit if you can. It should have a minimum of plasters and antiseptic wipes but consider also a bandage, tweezers and scissors. Other useful items are a torch and a whistle.

Picture courtesy of COSALT

Flotation suits can be real life savers for anglers both on shore and afloat.

General Information

Emergency Procedures: *What to do if things go wrong.*

If someone is shouting for help, waving one arm, showing orange smoke or a distress flare or an orange flag, blowing a whistle or flashing ... --- ... with a light, they are signalling that they are in trouble.

DO NOT ENTER THE WATER TO RESCUE ANYONE unless you are trained to carry out a rescue as this would put you also at risk.

If you are on a patrolled beach ask the Lifeguard for help, otherwise **call the Coastguard on 999**. Tell the operator what you have seen and the time and place of the incident. If possible get someone to remain at the scene while help is being summoned.

After you have called for help you may be able to assist the person in trouble by:

Shouting to reassure them - tell them to keep their arms in the water.

Using public rescue equipment if available.

Reaching out with a rod or landing net.

Throwing a rope or clothing tied together or something that will float.

When the casualty is out of the water keep them warm, administer first aid if possible and call for medical assistance if needed.

If You Get into Difficulties Yourself

Keep calm - *float on your back, keep your arms under water and breathe steadily.*
Do not exhaust yourself - *do not try to swim against the tide but head diagonally towards the shore if you can.*
Attract attention - *wave one arm only and shout for help.*

A full list of contact numbers for hazard advice and emergencies can be found at the end of the book

THIS GUIDE USES A RATING SYSTEM FOR ACCESSIBILITY TO AND COMFORT ON THE FISHING PLATFORMS

Ratings are given in the box on the right hand page for each venue. Use them to assess the suitability of the marks - the higher the number the more difficult the position.

ACCESSIBILITY
1: Suitable for the disabled angler
2: Short walk over light terrain.
3: Lengthy or strenuous walk over medium terrain
4: Lengthy walk over medium terrain with scramble to fishing platform.
5: Lengthy strenuous walk with scramble to fishing platform.

COMFORT
1: Promenade or pier.
2: Shingle or sand.
3: Boulder or stones possibly slippery.
4: Comfortable rock platform.
5: Uncomfortable rock platform.

These ratings are based on the author's own experience and are for guidance only. Conditions might be different on the day.

WHAT'S THE CATCH?

All these species are regularly caught in the area covered by this guide.

Cod

Three-bearded Rockling

Coalfish

Pollack

Ling

Whiting

Mackerel

Black Bream

Bass

Thick-lipped Grey Mullet

General Information

Thornback Ray

Spotted Ray

Bull Huss or Greater Spotted Dogfish

Plaice

Common Smoothound

Dab

Flounder

Conger Eel

Ballan Wrasse

Others species sometimes caught but not shown

Blonde Ray
Cuckoo Ray
Small-eyed Ray
Brill
Turbot

Cuckoo Wrasse
Herring
Tadpole Fish
Codling
Poor cod

Gurnard
Spurdog
Starry Smoothound
Tope

The record list of the Welsh Federation of Sea Anglers, Northern Region for these and many other species appears on page 93

TACKLE & BAIT

The choice of tackle soon becomes a matter of personal preference. Here the author gives his own views on the tackle that suits him when fishing in North Wales and Merseyside.

RODS

SHORE FISHING
The preferred rod for general beach and rock ledge shore fishing is a 13ft (3.9m) Conoflex Super Flick Tip made up of a 5ft (1.5m) carbon butt section to an 8ft (2.4m) tip. The relatively soft action suits the style of casting, sometimes called Lay Back, and the carbon end section beefs up the middle to provide power to deal with the likes of huss or conger.

REELS

My choice of reel has remained the same for 25 years and while ABU continues to produce Ambassadeur 7000 reels in all their shapes and forms I will keep using them. The reel itself is slightly heavier than many of the more recent brands on the market but this adds to its strength and durability allowing it to double as both a casting and medium boat reel, ideal for dinghy work.

LINE

MAIN LINE
For the past five years I have used Berkley Fireline for my boat and shore trips. The extra sensitivity over traditional monofilament lines, especially in bite detection is very impressive. Unfortunately it costs somewhere between 3 and 5 times the price of normal quality monofil and is less resistant to chafing over rough ground. On the plus side when used over clean ground it has a much longer life than monofil. Over heavy ground I use Daiwa Sensor Monofil, a traditional monofil which is good quality, not expensive and available in a wide range of strengths.

TERMINAL TACKLE
When making rigs I use Greased Weasel in 50 or 60lb (approx 25kg) breaking strain for the main trace body with hook lengths of 20 or 30lb (approx 12kg) breaking strain Amnesia.

HOOKS

I carry three patterns of hook in a variety of sizes. These are Mustad 3261 and Kamasan B940 Aberdeens which are ideal for worm baits while preferring the wider gape of the Mustad Viking 79515 for crab and fish baits.

BAIT

During the course of a year, expect to use up to a dozen different types of bait with the choice for each trip dependent on availablility, sea conditions, target species and the venue. The top four baits favoured by most anglers for boat and shore are peeler crab, lugworm, frozen sandeel and mackerel. Armed with all four any venue can be fished with confidence at any time of year. Certain venues sometimes require a different approach to bait and this information can be found in the bait section for each mark.

THE RIG GUIDE

TWO-HOOK PATERNOSTER
Also called a 1-up, 1-down, this is probably the most popular rig with shore anglers in Britain. Baits can be fished either one above and one below the lead or both above, covering different depths. It can be streamlined for distance casting by including bait clips.

ROTTEN BOTTOM
Reduce fish losses from the lead snagging on rough ground by using a "rotten bottom" rig. This rig has a length of line with a lower breaking strain included just above the lead. This weaker line will break before the main line when the lead fouls, losing the lead but keeping the fish.

• • • • • • • • • • • • • • • *General Information* • •
The Main Systems used in this Guide

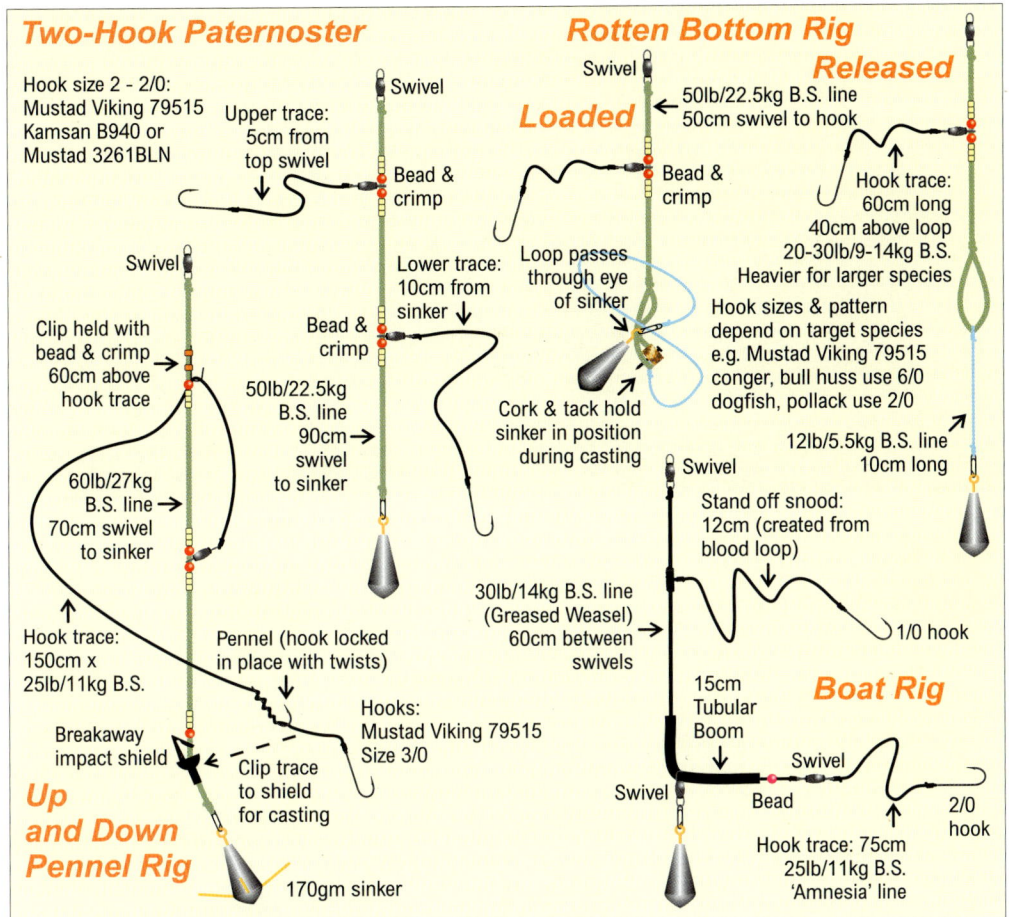

UP AND DOWN RIG
Catches of cod or ray can be improved with a long trace fished below the lead but this is not aerodynamic and can foul during a cast. The method shown eliminates both problems. This rig needs a resonable tide run to take the trace away from the main line to avoid tangles.

BOAT RIG
Like the paternoster, this rig allows bait to be offered at different depths. Vary the line strengths and hook sizes to target a wide range of species. The hollow plastic tubular boom is to prevent the bottom trace fouling with the main trace in slow tidal runs.

PWLLHELI

A venue well known for specimen bull huss

A big bull huss from Pwllheli beach

The beach at Pwllheli lies between Abersoch and Portmadoc on the southern coast of the Lleyn peninsula. The beach itself stretches from Gimblet Rock in the east to the headland north of Llanbedrog in the west but due to access is mainly fished only as far west as the golf course. The steep shingle bank offers a good depth of water over high water and is becoming increasingly popular as a match venue, recently playing host to the SAMF Masters.

How to get There

From Caernarfon follow the A487 to the A499 which takes you into Pwllheli. Follow signs for Abersoch before turning left at the mini roundabout/pedestrian crossing just after the station. Carry on along this road past the harbour before turning left opposite the Victoria Hotel for the harbour and eastern beach marks or straight on for the more western marks.

What & When

At the start of the year catches are usually small to medium sized whiting, dabs and a few dogfish with the odd spotted ray putting in an appearance in early March. During April specimen bull huss move within casting range while dogfish increase in numbers. Thornback ray show in May and specimens above the 10lb (4.5kg) mark are taken every year. Bags during summer usually consist of dogfish,

Mid Wales Largest Tackle Shop
Aber Fishing Tackle Shop,
3 Terrace Rd, Aberystwyth, SY23 1NY
(Opposite Wethespoons). Tel 01970 611200

Live & Frozen Bait available
Permits for Local Rivers and Lakes

FISHING
(Local Fishing Information)

Free Food
Free Sea Fishing
Feed your family for Free
Buy a complete Rod, Reel & Line from only £29.99 and catch your own fish for FREE

Tackle Shop open on Sundays during Summer

Fly Rod & Reel Deals from £35.00

Fishing Flies for local River, Lake & Sea Fishing at Shop
Visit our 2 websites
www.flymail.com
www.flymailflies.co.uk

SHORE FISHING around Aberystwyth, Clarach, Borth & Ynyslas

Zone A
Sandy Beach
Method of Fishing - Ledgering
Baits - Ragworm, Lugworm, Razor Fish, Sand Eels, Mackerel Strips & Crabs
Fish Species - Flounders, Dabs, Bass, Ray Species & Dogfish.

Zone B
Rocky Coastline
Method of Fishing - Ledgering, Float Fishing, Spinning
Baits - Prawns, Ragworm, Sand Eels, Razor Fish, Crab also Spinning with Plugs, Tobys & Flying C
Fish Species - Bass, Mackerel, Wrasse, Rockling

Zone C
Shelving Species
Method - Ledgering, Spinning, Float
Baits - Razor Fish, Ragworm, Mackerel, Sand Eel, Crab, Squid, Lugworm
Species - Bass, Flounders, Ray Species, Dogfish, Wrasse, Conger, Pollock, Dabs, Mackerel, Bull Huss.

Fishing Tackle on 1st Floor. Travel Luggage, Handbags, Wallets, Welsh Gifts etc. On Ground Floor. Parking nearby, available opposite Tackle Shop at Iceland & Lidl Store Car Park

SEA FISHING BOATS FOR HIRE FROM ABERYSTWYTH HARBOUR
Harbourmaster Tel: 01970 611433
Marina Tel: 01970 611422
www.aberystwythmarina.com

Lady Jane	Sean Roche
01544 388492	07973 215106
Ma Chipe	Mike Harris
01970 623465	07870351295

Live and Frozen Bait available from Fishing Tackle Shop, 3 Terrace Rd., Aberystwyth Tel: 01970 611200 (opposite to Aberystwyth Railway Station)

RIVERS & LAKES
River Rheidol	No.1
River Ystwyth	No.2
Talybont Lakes	No.3
Dinas reservoir	No.4
Nantymoch	No.5
Llyn Craig Y Pistyll	No.6
Blaenmelindwr	No..7
Syfrydin	No.8
Rhosgoch	No.9
Trisant Lakes	No.10
Teifi Pools	No.11
Fron Fishery	No.12
Oerfa Lake	No.13

Permits for above areas from
ABER FISHING TACKLE SHOP
Aberystwyth Tel. 01970 611200
www.aberystwythdirectory.com
www.flymail.com
Please call in to the
Fishing Tackle Shop
(opposite Wetherspoons)
for up to date information.

Permits available from **ABER FISHING TACKLE SHOP**
3 Terrace Rd., Aberystwyth. Tel: 01970 611200
(Opposite Wetherspoons above The Bag Shop)
Fax: 01970 611062   Email: flymailuk@aol.com
Full Range of **FISHING TACKLE** in stock. See our wide range plus Fishing Flies available at the above address. Fresh and Frozen bait is available from the Tackle Shop

Location of Aber Fishing Tackle Shop
3 Terrace Rd., Aberystwyth SY23 1NY
Tel: 01970 611200

For further extensive local information please visit our website www.aberystwythdirectory.com

ROD LICENCES 2012

Anyone aged 12 or over who fishes for Salmon, Trout, Freshwater Fish or Eels in England or Wales must have an Environment Agency Rod Fishing Licence
Telephone : 08708 506 506

	Non Migratory Trout & Coarse Fish	Salmon & Sea Trout
Full	£ 27.00	£ 72.00
Concessionary	£ 18.00	£ 48.00
8 Day	£ 10.00	£ 23.00
1 Day	£ 3.75	£ 8.00
Junior	£ 5.00	£ 5.00

ABERYSTWYTH ANGLING ASSOCIATION - Rheidol River

LOCAL SEASON - ADULT	£ 100.00	VISITOR - ADULT	£ 150.00	Visitor Weekly - Adult	£ 84.00
LOCAL SEASON - COUPLES	£ 132.00	VISITOR - (Joint Husband & Wife)	£ 180.00	Visitor Weekly - Concession	£ 72.00
LOCAL SEASON - OAP	£ 70.00	VISITOR - (Concessionary)	£ 100.00	Visitor Weekly - Under 16	£ 15.00
LOCAL SEASON - OAP COUPLES	£ 95.00	VISITOR(Concession Husband & Wife)	£ 130.00		Local Residents for Rivers
LOCAL SEASON - UNDER 16	£ 22.00	VISITOR - SEASON - OAP	£ 92.00		All Waters only
LOCAL SEASON - STUDENTS	£ 72.50	VISITOR - SEASON - (Youth)	£ 22.00	Daily - Adult £ 20.00	£15.00
BOAT - SEASON (Deposit £10.00)				Daily - Concession £ 15.00	£12.00

LOCAL means possessing a Ceredigion Council Tax Bill for their local dwelling
Secretary: Mike Barret 01970 623682 Email: mbarrettu05k@yahoo.co.uk

LLANILAR ANGLING ASSOCIATION - Ystwyth River

		Visitor - Non Residents	
LOCAL SEASON - ADULT	£ 30.00	Visitor Season - Adult	£ 54.00
LOCAL SEASON - OAP	£ 20.00	Visitor Season - Pensioner	£ 29.00
LOCAL SEASON - UNDER 16	£ 10.00	Visitor Season - Under 16	£ 19.00
LOCAL SEASON - UNDER 11(primary School)	£ 3.00	Weekly - Adult	£ 34.00
		Weekly - Under 16	£ 16.00
		Daily - Adult	£ 17.00
		Daily - Under 16	£ 8.00

LOCAL means possessing a Ceredigion Council Tax Bill for their local dwelling
Secretary: John Astill Tel: 01974 261237

TALYBONT LAKES

| SEASON | £ 45.00 | Lakes. Fly Fishing only for Brown Trout on Dwfn, Conach and Penrhaedr |
| DAY TICKET | £ 10.00 | Fly Fishing and worming for Brown Trout in Nant-Y-Cagal |

Secretary: Mr. M. Williams 01974 251330

TREGARON ANGLING ASSOCIATION

				River only or Llyn Berwyn only or Teifi Pools (Teifi, Egnant and Hir) only			
				Day, All Waters - Everyone £13.00			
SEASON - ADULT	£140.00	SEASON - ADULT	£ 80.00	OAP		£10.00	
SEASON - OAP	£ 105.50	SEASON - OAP	£ 63.00	16 to 18		£7.00	
SEASON - 16 - 18	£ 70.00	SEASON - 16 - 18	£ 35.00	One Water	£75.00		
SEASON - UNDER 16	£ 35.00	SEASON - UNDER 16	£ 20.00	OAP	£55.00		
				16 to 18	£38.00		

Secretary: Cheryl Burman 01974 298177

DINAS 1st. April to 31st.October (Brown Trout 17th.October)
Fly, Spinning, Worm Ledgered or with float, Brown & Rainbow Trout

Season (8 Fish Limit)	£ 250.00
Day Permit (8 Fish) - Adult	£ 14.00
Day Permit & Under 16 & Pensioners	£ 7.50
Evening Permit (from 4.30pm. 4 Fish)	£ 7.50
Family (15 Fish Limit)	£ 33.00
Winter Fishing Season	£ 30.00
Winter Season Day	£ 6.00

NANTYMOCH - Season 1st. April to 30th. September

Fly Fishing only (Brown Trout)
| Season Permits (6 Fish per day limit) | £ 60.00 |
| Day Permits (6 Fish Limit) | £ 6.00 |

Opens 0700 - 22.00   Sunday 08.00 - 22.00

Tickets from BP Petrol station, Ponterwyd 01970 890649

OTHER FISHING IN THE ABERYSTWYTH AREA INCLUDE THE FOLLOWING

4Trec Fishing, Pantyffynnon, Bontgoch, Talybont,	Tel. 01970 832291
Fron Trout Fishery, Bontnewydd, Near Bronant, Aberystwyth,	Tel. 01974 251392
Cwm Nant Fishery Golf Course, Capel Bangor, Aberystwyth	Tel. 01970 880239 See Map on reverse No.15
Tair Llyn Coarse Fishery, Tair Llyn, Cwm Rheidol, Aberystwyth	Tel. 01970 880560 See Map on reverse No.14
Troed Y Bryn Fishery, Cribyn, Near Lampeter	Tel. 01570 470798

Shore Marks

huss, various rays and small whiting with black bream, garfish and gurnard also taken regularly. Mackerel shoals often work well within casting range during settled spells and provide exciting sport on light gear. The summer and early autumn is also more productive for fishing the harbour mouth as black bream, flounder and bass move in to feed. The bream and flounder can run up to 2lb 8oz (1.1kg) while most of the bass are under 3lb (1.35kg). Larger fish are caught every year especially on plugs or spinners fished at dawn or dusk when the harbour is quieter. Whiting numbers increase at the end of September and with dogfish, dabs and the odd ray provide most of the sport to the year's end.

How to Catch Them

The main beach is usually more productive over high water especially after dark but with a good depth of water some excellent catches have been recorded during the day. The fish are usually found within 100m of the tide line but on occasion a longer cast can pay off. The harbour mouth will produce steadily throughout the flood although the first two hours of the ebb are often better. Long distance casting is not required here as an 80 yard cast at high water will put your bait in the main channel and amongst the fish. Boating activity during the holidays and at weekends can be a problem so time your session to coincide with dawn or dusk.

TACKLE.
A 2-hook rig loaded with size 2 to 4/0 dependent on bait size and target species is the accepted method but if the fish are scarce a change to a 1-hook rig clipped down for extra distance can often pay off. As the tide run is fairly light a 4 or 5oz (130 to 150g) lead will hold bottom although a breakaway lead is required during onshore blows due to the undertow. In these conditions floating weed can also be a problem. In the harbour mouth the tide is a lot stronger but while there is no weed in the water the mark can be fished on all but the biggest tides. The same rig used for the main beach will work here but as the target species are flounder, black bream and small bass look to be using hooks in the size 2 to 1/0 range.

BAIT.
From the main beach worm, sandeel, razor fish and mackerel strip will cater for the majority of fish but peeler crab is more or less essential when fishing the harbour mouth.

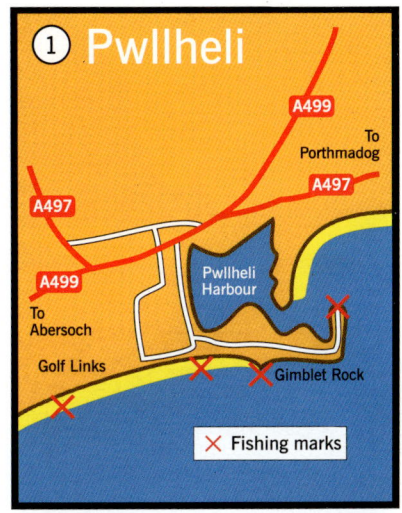

O.S Map Sheet No. 123
Admiralty Chart No. 1512
High water: Liverpool −3hr 07
Access: 2 Comfort: 2
(See ratings at foot of page 7)

STAR CATCH
The Welsh Shore Record bull huss was caught here in May 1992. The captor was G.C Ebbs from Norfolk and the fish scaled 19lb 14oz (9.0kg).

HELL'S MOUTH / PORTH NEIGWL

A classic storm beach

Situated on the south west tip of the Lleyn Peninsula this is a prolific storm beach. The beach is framed by the headlands at Rhiw and Cilan and by steep clay cliffs along most of its length. High water washes the foot of the cliffs on spring tides and, with an onshore blow, neap tides so it is no coincidence that the main access points are at areas which can be fished over high water. The seabed from beyond the low water mark to the shingle foreshore is mainly sand and a few stones with boulders and kelp below the headlands.

How to get There

From Caernarfon take the A487 and then the A499 to Abersoch via Pwllheli. From Abersoch follow the signs to Hell's Mouth passing through Llanegan before parking in the layby at the south eastern end of the beach. From there it is a comfortable 5 minute walk to the beach but allow a further 15 minutes to the marks under Cilan Head now that access through Nant Farm has been stopped. Access to the marks at the northern end of the beach is via a footpath and a steep set of steps near the camp site at Rhiw.

What & When

Sport is slow early in the year and not until April do dogfish and a few school bass make travel

Fine small-eyed ray at 10lb 8oz (4.73kg) from Hell's Mouth

from the main conurbations worthwhile. Better sized bass in the 3 to 6lb range (1.35 to 2.7kg), can be taken from May to October with the possibility of specimens to 10lb (4.5kg). Wrasse, rockling and small bull huss can also be expected from the rougher ground then with small turbot, mackerel, coalfish and whiting from the main beach. Rays, in particular small eyed, are sometimes taken with some larger specimen fish found in October and November when whiting, coalfish, dabs and school bass are at their most prolific.

How to Catch Them

The best times are from low water up the tide for 1½ hours and then again when the water reaches the shingle over high water for 2 hours of the ebb. Although fish will be taken on neaps the best tides are those between 8.5 and 9.2m at Liverpool. Larger tides than this wash the cliffs so the clay discolours the water with detrimental effect.

BAIT

The top three baits on this beach are crab (peeler and soft back), sandeel and, when a surf is running, razor fish. There are a few crab among the rocks below Cilan Head but it can be hard work to collect enough for a session so it pays to bring a supply. Sandeel isn't a problem since frozen is almost as productive as fresh. Razor fish can be dug at Abersoch on low waters of less than 0.6m at Liverpool.

TACKLE

For the main beach a 1- or 2-hook rig fished above the weight is ideal. Hook is size dependent on bait size and target species but a good all round hook would be a 3/0 Aberdeen or similar. During calm conditions a plain lead is all that is required whilst a grip lead in the 6 to 7oz (150 to 170g) range is necessary to get the distance and hold bottom in a surf. Fishing the rough ground requires a different approach and the rotten bottom rig illustrated in the tackle and bait section is to be preferred. This area of rough ground will also produce bass on plugs.

⚠ SAFETY ANGLE

Be careful when wading because the undertow can be very strong. Make sure that if you intend to fish over high water that the tide doesn't cut off your exit from the beach.

•• Shore Marks ••

② Porth Neigwl/ Hell's Mouth

O.S Map Sheet No. 123
Admiralty Chart No. 1512
High water: Liverpool −3hr 17
Beach: Access: 2 Comfort: 2
Rocks: Access: 3 Comfort: 3
(See ratings at foot of page 7)

❄ TOP TIP

This beach fishes best in a moderate surf. A west to south westerly breeze force 3 or 4 is ideal. Floating weed can be a problem but keeping the rod tip high and reducing the amount of line in the water helps.

UWCHMYNYDD

A challenging mark with the prospect of specimen fish

Located on the south west tip of the Lleyn Peninsula overlooking Bardsey Island are the rock edges of Uwchmynydd. Fishing is from these rocks over a sea bed of rock and kelp with patchy sand at distance.

How to Get There

From Caernarfon take the A487 then the A499 joining the B4417 just past Trefor. Stay on this road to its junction with the B4413 which will take you into Aberdaron. Carry on out of the village up the steep hill that overlooks the beach then turn left at the chapel. This narrow road leads after a mile or so to a National Trust car park leaving a 15 minute fairly strenuous walk down the valley to the rock ledges.

What & When

January to March is a fairly productive time of the year with pollack in the 1 to 3lb (0.45 to 1.35kg) range, dogfish, whiting, specimen 3-bearded rockling and the odd codling making up the bulk of bags. Coalfish, small ling, tadpole fish and a suprising number of conger in the 5 to 15lb (2.25 to 6.75kg) range can also be anticipated. Bull huss start to make their presence felt from the start of April staying until early winter, the better specimens, some topping 13lb (5.9kg), showing early in the season rather than later. April sees ballan wrasse increasing in numbers and along with pollack and mackerel make up the bulk of catches during the summer days with bull huss, rockling, dogfish and conger after dark. Whiting and codling return during October replacing the departing mackerel and wrasse but the remainder of the species mentioned stay throughout the winter. Other less prolific summer visitors include spotted ray, smoothhound, plaice and mullet.

How to Catch Them

Tides between the mainland at Uwchmynydd and Bardsey Island are fast and as a consequence neap tides are the friendliest to fish. If you do have to fish the larger springs aim to fish a couple of hours either side of the low water period when the run of the tide is not as strong.

Shore Marks

> ## ⚠ SAFETY ANGLE
>
> *Facing south west and into the prevailing winds, the rock edges become dangerous in winds over force 4 from the south to west quadrant. Even on relatively calm days the tidal overfalls in Bardsey Sound will often send freak waves crashing over rocks that otherwise appear to be well above the reach of the sea.*

③ Uwchmynydd

BAIT
Throughout the winter months the two top baits are sandeel and mackerel with peeler crab useful during the summer. Other baits likely to score are fresh whiting for conger and bull huss, and squid but worm baits in my experience are unproductive and when peeler crab is available, not worth using.

TACKLE
When fishing the rougher ground it pays to fish a single hook rig comprising a "rotten bottom" which will reduce tackle and fish losses by lessening the chance of the sinker and second hook fouling on retrieval. Hook size depends on quarry, for the smaller fish like wrasse, dogfish and pollack choose a size 1/0 to 2/0 stepping up to size 5/0 and 6/0 for bull huss and conger. Hook pattern and strength are also important so see the Tackle section for a guide.

O.S. Map Sheet No. 123
Admiralty Chart No. 1971
High water: Liverpool −3hr 20
Access: 5 Comfort: 4
(See ratings at foot of page 7)

*Mick Duff with a 9lb 12oz (4.4kg)
Bull Huss from Uwchmynydd*

⭐ STAR CATCH
On 23 April 1987 Mike Robinson of Llandudno landed a bull huss weighing 15lb 7oz (6.89kg) while fishing at Uwchmynydd.

WHISTLING SANDS / PORTHOER

An often under-rated venue having excellent shelter, deep water and good fishing

Lying on the north coast of the Lleyn Peninsula, a couple of miles from its southern tip, is the small beach of Porthoer, also known as Whistling Sands. The bay is flanked on three sides by steep cliffs offering excellent protection from winds from northeast through to the southwest quadrant. The beach itself is comprised of coarse sand interspersed with the odd rock outcrop and, being fairly steep, offers a good depth of water to a moderate cast.

How to Get There

From Caernarfon take the A499 before turning onto the B4417, approximately 13 miles. This road passes through Nefyn and Tudweiliog before it joins the B4413 (signposted Aberdaron). Travel along the B4413 for a mile before taking the right hand turn at the sign for Porthoer which lies three miles further on. Parking is available above the beach which is reached down a narrow private track. Parking is £3 per day but free for members of the National Trust. Vehicles are not allowed access beyond the car park.

What & When

Porthoer is often regarded as a second choice venue, visited only when the more recognised beaches in the area are unfishable, but it deserves a greater recognition in its own right. During the first few months of the year the beach plays host to a variety of small flatfish, school bass and coalfish. As spring gives way to summer dogfish, coalfish and bass are the dominant species but owing to the beaches popularity with holidaymakers it is more advisable to fish after dark. If this is not possible then the rock edges at either end of the beach offer wrasse, pollack and dogfish during the daylight hours. Autumn brings better coalfish and also the chance of a decent sized bass when a surf is running. Whiting and small codling can also be expected as the sea temperature starts to drop later in the season. The tides are not really an issue at this venue although the influence of the Tripod Bank and its overfalls, a mile or so offshore, can create a left to right drift during the first couple of hours of the flood.

Shore Marks

How to Catch Them

The beach fishes best either side of low water then over high when a short cast after dark can often find coalfish and school bass feeding in the back wash.

Spinning during the summer months from the rocks on the left hand side across the mouth of the bay with a small lure such as a Mepps can be productive for launce (greater sandeel) and mackerel

TACKLE

A 1-up 1-down rig fished at 80m will score well at this venue but don't be afraid to fish at close range especially after dark. A 6 or 7oz (150 to 170g) plain lead will hold bottom comfortably except when there is a surf running when grips are required to counter the lateral drift. When fishing the main beach a 1-up 1-down rig is effective but the rougher ground either side of the bay can warrant the use of a rotten bottom rig if the cleaner ground cannot be reached.

BAIT

Sandeel can be dug or scraped from the sand after dark from the low water mark and a few razor fish can be collected over low water on the big spring tides (less than 0.5m at Liverpool). Both are excellent baits here and both can be frozen and used later without a great difference in performance. Peeler crab is the other main bait particularly for bass and coalfish.

Phil Simpson with a Ballan Wrasse caught from the rock edges at Porthoer

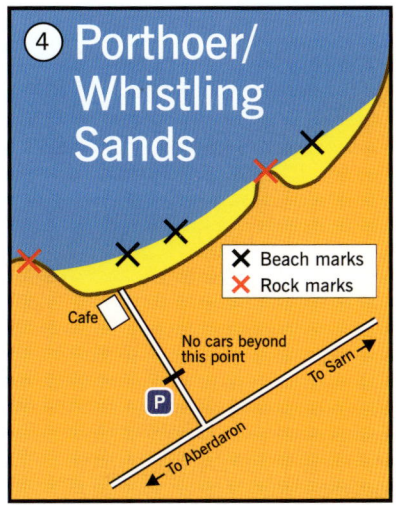

④ Porthoer/ Whistling Sands

O.S. Map Sheet No. 123
Admiralty Chart No. 1971
High water: Liverpool –3hr 20
Access: 3 Comfort: 2
(See ratings at foot of page 7)

❗ SAFETY ANGLE

A pleasant and inviting beach venue but an onshore wind during high water springs often pushes the tide right up to the clay cliffs and can cut off unwary anglers.

PISTYLL

A rock platform to reach rays and the hounds

Pistyll Point lies a few miles north east of Nefyn on the north coast of the Lleyn Peninsula. It is a fairly comfortable rock mark on the point offering a sandy bottom straight out with rough ground either side.

How to Get There

From Caernarfon take the A487 Porthmadog road for 3 miles before joining the A499. 10 miles further on turn right on to the B4417 (sign posted Nefyn) passing through Llithfaen before reaching the village of Pistyll. There are two main points of access to the venue: from the beach below the caravan park at Wern or, with permission and a small donation in the charity box, through Tir Bach Farm above the headland. The latter is more direct but the the path is beginning to erode so care must be taken and it can only be used during the summer months when the small camp site is open.

What & When

From January to March catches consist mainly of whiting, dabs, coalfish and the occasional codling. In years gone by this period of the year used to boast a run of spurdog but sadly commercial pressure during the 1970's reduced their numbers to such an extent that they are now a rarity. Smoothhound can provide exciting sport after dark during May and June with spotted and small eyed ray featuring on occasion. Crab baits fished at short range over the rough ground can produce the occasional bass. Dogfish are present from March through to December and such are their numbers that on occasion it becomes impossible to avoid them. The end of September sees an influx of whiting mainly around the 12oz (0.3kg) mark but some have topped the 2lb (0.9kg) mark. Dabs will also show as will codling, especially when the sea is coloured and calming down after a blow. Other species that can be expected during the year are bull huss, some topping the 12lb mark, grey gurnard, plaice and mackerel.

How to Catch Them

Facing northwest the mark is sheltered from winds from south round to northeast but becomes unfishable in anything above a force 4 from the west to northerly quadrant.

Shore Marks

TACKLE

The tide run is moderate on spring tides an can easily be fished with a 150 or 170g grip lead. Distance casting is useful at this venue and a 2-hook rig clipped down works well. Hook size depends on target species but generally a size 2/0 in the stronger patterns like the Kamasan B940 or Mustad 9172LBR will take the smaller fish and have enough strength for the larger species. During the summer float fishing into a ground bait trail can be very effective for mackerel, launce, small pollack and the occasional bass.

BAIT

Sandeel scores heavily throughout the year and only takes a back seat to crab during the early summer when the smoothhound are running and later in the year when after codling and coalfish. Lugworm and mussel can also work well at this time of year with mackerel strip tops for whiting.

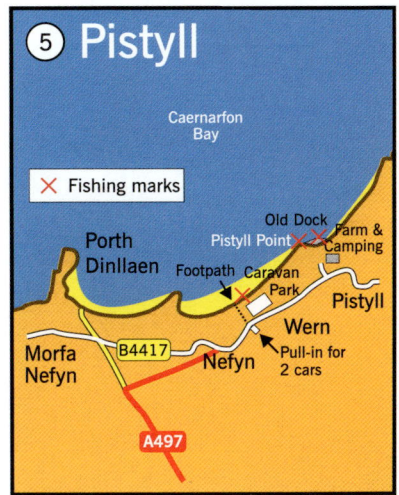

A small spotted ray on a night with no dogfish.

O.S. Map Sheet No. 123
Admiralty Chart No. 1971
High water: Liverpool −2hr 00
Access: 4 Comfort: 4
(See ratings at foot of page 7)

❄ TOP TIP

The rising tide will gradually wash away ground bait placed at different levels above the low water mark releasing a steady controlled bait trail into the sea.

DINAS DINLLE

Plenty of whiting and some good bass during the summer

Dinas Dinlle is a classic storm beach situated at the southern entrance to the Menai Strait. Before the decline of the fishery it used to boast some of the finest bass fishing in the British Isles. The beach consists of a shingle bank which gives way to sand from half tide down. The sand is interlaced with shifting gullies and banks the positions of which can change almost overnight. This is especially marked with an onshore wind is coupled to a spring tide so it pays to arrive early in the flood to inspect the beach.

How to Get There

Take the Caernarfon turn-off from the A55 Expressway. Once through Caernarfon follow signs to Pwllheli for 6 miles before taking a right turn, sign posted Dinas Dinlle. The beach is 1½ miles along this road. Parking is available at various points along the road which runs parallel to the beach. Access beyond this point is by foot and, due to the shingle, quite arduous.

What & When

A storm beach which can take a heavy surf especially during a blow from the west. It can be unfishable in anything more than a force 5 from this quadrant. A south westerly breeze around force 3 or 4 gives ideal conditions. Silk weed gathering on the leader knot can be a problem in early autumn but becomes less trouble as the season progresses. Early season sport consists of whiting, coalfish and codling with the best results when there is some movement and colour in the water. The whiting are around 1lb (0.45kg) with codling in the 2 to 4lb (0.9 to 1.8kg) range. School bass start to appear during March and with dogfish and coalfish make most of the sport through to May when better sized bass arrive. Bass and dogfish are the two main species throughout summer with bull huss and thornback ray taken on occasion. As September gives way to October whiting move within casting range and good bags can be expected after dark. The school bass remain until December with codling and coalfish showing in reasonable numbers from October to the year's end.

Shore Marks

How to Catch Them

The best time to fish Dinas is on spring tides from 3 hours before to 3 hours after high water, even better if the majority of this period falls in darkness.

BAIT
During the winter months sandeel works well for whiting and dogfish with codling and coalfish favouring crab, lugworm, mussel or razor fish. Peeler crab is usually the top bait in the summer although fresh mackerel can be productive when the huss and thornback are running.

TACKLE
Due to the topography of the beach the ability to put a bait out a good distance can be useful especially when searching out a distant gully. However, on most occasions a 80 yard cast will suffice and over the high water period fish are often found working the gully at the base of the shingle. 1-up 1-down rigs are the most commonly used end tackle, varying hook size to suit the species available. A range of hooks from size 1 to size 3/0 will cover most needs. 5oz (140g) breakaway leads will cope with most conditions. Heavier leads are needed to counteract the tide run when long lining large fish baits, intended for thornback ray, back from the low water mark.

This 30lb (13.5kg) cod was a surprise catch at Dinas Dinlle

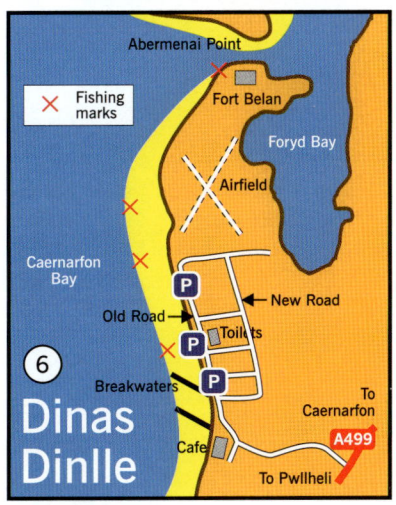

O.S. Map Sheet No. 123
Admiralty Chart No. 1970
High water: Liverpool −1hr 20
Access: 2 Comfort: 2
(See ratings at foot of page 7)

✸ TOP TIP

Low water is surprisingly unproductive and is only worth attention if the quarry is thornback and even then don't anticipate action until the tide reaches the shingle.

CAERNARFON

Easy access and good sport on light tackle

Directly under the castle walls at Caernarfon at the mouth of the River Seiont. The river spills into the Menai Strait at the bridge and forms channels that run either side of the sand bar at the mouth of the estuary.

How to Get There

From the A55 Expressway take the Caernarfon exit and join the A499. Immediately before entering the town turn right at the roundabout and follow the signs for the Castle. There is parking on the quay near the swing bridge and also in front of the marina at Victoria Dock. Both spots leave a short comfortable walk to the marks which start at the swing bridge. If fishing the marks to the west of the harbour turn right at the roundabout half a mile past Caernarfon following the signs to Is Helen.

What & When

Mostly small codling from the start of the year through to the end of March but as the first crab moult of the year gets underway so the fishing improves. Flounders provide most of the sport with a high proportion over the 1lb

There are some great flatfish to be caught at Caernarfon. Here Alun Jones shows a 1lb 15oz (0.87kg) flounder.

Shore Marks

Fishing directly off the quay where you can park and with level access right up to the comfortable marks, Caernarfon castle is an ideal location for anglers with limited mobility.

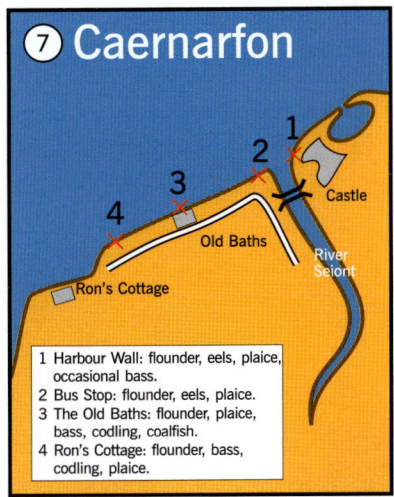

⑦ Caernarfon

1 Harbour Wall: flounder, eels, plaice, occasional bass.
2 Bus Stop: flounder, eels, plaice.
3 The Old Baths: flounder, plaice, bass, codling, coalfish.
4 Ron's Cottage: flounder, bass, codling, plaice.

(0.45kg) mark and many nudging 2lb (0.9kg). Coalfish and eels are also fairly common with plaice and bass putting in an occasional appearance. May and June offer the best results although October can produce the better sized flounder. Codling in the 2 to 3lb (0.9 to 1.35kg) range can be expected during the autumn especially on the bend towards the dock entrance.

How to Catch Them

The channel below the castle walls can be reached with a short cast and although the opposite channel is as equally productive the former is preferred purely for comfort and ease of access. The sea bed west of the harbour and down past the old swimming baths to the cottage is predominately small stones and mud with patches of weed so occasional tackle losses can be expected.

BAIT
Worm baits can be productive early and late in the year but from April to September then peeler crab which can be collected locally, has no equal.

TACKLE
As the bottom in the harbour mouth is relatively clear and the tidal flow is gentle then light tackle can be used. A small multiplier loaded with 10lb line matched to a light bass rod is ideal. When fishing the swimming pool area step up the gear to take into account the rougher bottom and faster tide flow.

METHOD
For best results fish the channel on the flood and early ebb allowing the sinker to roll in the tide. A simple flowing trace to a size 1/0 hook, preferably a heavier gauge like the Kamasan B940, will not only pick up the flounders but also be strong enough should you hit into a larger fish such as a bass. The shore to the west of the harbour is best fished on the first 2 hours of the flood and then again 2 hours before high water and 1 hour after.

O.S. Map Sheet No. 114
Admiralty Chart No. 1464
High water: Liverpool −1hr 18
Prom: Access: 1 Comfort: 1
Beach: Access: 2 Comfort: 2
(See ratings at foot of page 7)

STAR CATCH

In May 1998, local man Elwyn Hughes caught a 3lb 0oz (1.35kg) flounder at Caernarfon.

THE SWELLIES

Exciting all weather fishing in some of the strongest currents around Britain

The Menai Strait separates Anglesey from the mainland and has some of the strongest tides in Britain. The section between the bridges, known as the Swellies, has very strong currents flowing up to 8 knots on spring tides. The bottom is rocky ledges swathed in kelp interspersed with reefs and gravel. It is flanked on both sides by steep wooded banks so access can be a problem. Sheltered from every quarter the Swellies is a true all weather mark.

How to Get There

To reach the venue, take the Bangor turn off the A55 Expressway and follow the signs for Holyhead. Immediately before crossing the Suspension Bridge take a left hand turn towards the University gardens. Access to the shore is via the large metal gate adjacent to the bridge or through the trees further along the road.

What & When

The most productive time is a couple of hours either side of the low water slack water, about 4 hours after high water at Liverpool. There is another slack water period around high water, about 2 hours before high water at Liverpool but large tides can drive you into the trees. There are a number of good marks, some favourites being:

1) The flat ledges opposite Swellie Rock, less snaggy than other spots and fishes well for coalfish, codling and with relatively shallow water offers a better chance of bass.

2) The Boat House Point a couple of hundred metres east of Swellie Rock. Due to the topography a back eddy forms on the east flowing flood which allows the mark to fished when those nearby are unfishable due to strength of the run. The sea bed is fairly rough and conger are often taken by those prepared to specialise.

3) Although not in the Swellies proper, another good mark lies just past the beacon a couple of hundred m to the east of the Suspension Bridge. An 80m cast will find 50ft (15m) of water, which holds a fair head of codling during the autumn months. The mark is best fished during the last 2 hours of the west flowing run as it soon becomes unfishable on the easterly run due to the funnelling effect of the bridge.

Shore Marks

Bass like this are a big attraction at the Swellies.

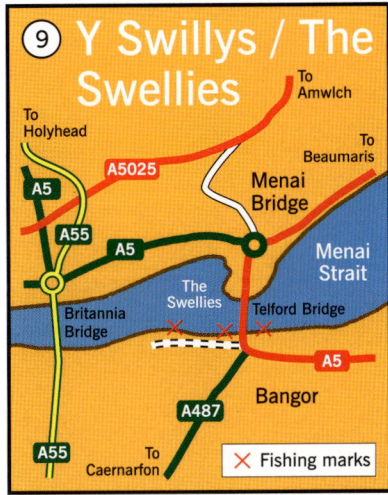

O.S. Map Sheet No. 114
Admiralty Chart No. 1464
High water: Liverpool –0hr 30
Access: 3 Comfort: 3
(See ratings at foot of page 7)

The Swellies is very quiet until May when codling start to show. Most of the fish are around 12 in (30cm) but a few larger fish to 2lb 8oz (1.1kg) can be taken. They stay throughout the summer increasing in numbers and size as autumn approaches by when they average around 2lb (0.9kg) although larger fish around 3 to 4lb (1.35 to 1.8kg) are sometimes taken. Coalfish also show in good numbers during the autumn with 1 to 2lb (0.45 to 0.9kg) fish the norm. Bass can be taken from June to September with the better specimens falling to large crab baits fished close in amongst the rock ledges. Quiet early morning sessions produce the best results. Conger also feature in catches and although the majority are straps around 5 to 12lb (2.25 to 5.4kg), larger fish are often hooked and lost.

How to Catch Them

BAIT

Throughout the year peeler crab or soft back crab is the most productive bait for bass and cod. Butterfish collected locally will sometimes tempt bass and cod with conger favouring a side of freshly caught fish.

TACKLE

Not a place for the faint hearted with stout rods and heavy multipliers loaded with 30lb (13.5kg) BS line the order of the day. A rotten bottom to a 6oz (170g) grip lead will minimise losses as will fine wire Aberdeen hooks. These tend to bend out of the kelp stalks which are the reason for the majority of tackle losses. Size 3/0 to 6/0 are recommended.

BANGOR PIER

Sheltered, comfortable and very easy to reach

Bangor Pier extends from the mainland side into the Menai Strait. The seabed on the left hand side of the pier is comprised of mud, small stones and mussel but becomes predominantly sand at the pier head. The Strait offers excellent shelter from all weathers with only the comfort factor to take into consideration.

How to Get There

Leave the A55 Expressway at the Bangor exit and follow the road into Bangor turning down towards the Pier immediately after Dickies Boatyard. There is plenty of parking space by the pier gates and a limited number of free spaces on the road itself.

What & When

Results are disappointing early in the year with just undersized codling and the odd flatfish showing. The main moult of shore crab early in May sees sport improve with flounders, school bass and a few sizeable codling moving in. Coalfish, small pollack, mackerel and dabs add to the established fish during the summer months. Plaice start to appear in late Spring with sport peaking early in October. Whiting can also be expected along with pout, dabs, coalfish and the occasional dogfish. The left hand side of the pier between the first two kiosks is regarded as the hot spot producing a lot of plaice over the 1lb 8oz (0.7kg) mark along with several fish a season nudging 3lb (1.35kg). Codling start to show in good numbers at this time and although they only average around the 1lb 8oz (0.7kg) to 2lb (0.9kg) bracket they can be plentiful on occasion especially from the right hand kiosk at the pier head. Whiting can also be expected along with pout and dabs. Results remain consistent until early December when sport tails away as "snow melt" from the nearby mountains enters the Strait. Night sessions can be very productive during autumn and early winter but access has to be arranged with the pier warden, see box right.

How to Catch Them

The tidal effect is negligible around the mid sections of the pier although grip leads will required during the worst of the run when fishing the pier head. Best results are had a couple of hours either side of high tide

• • Shore Marks • •

Built in 1886 and restored in 1988, Bangor Pier has smooth, level access right up to the marks and is ideal for anglers with limited mobility. It even has toilets for the disabled.

BAIT
Peeler crab is essential during the spring through to early Autumn with lug and rag scoring later in the winter. Mussel can also be very effective later in the year especially when offered as a cocktail with worm.

TACKLE
A 1-up 1-down rig with size 1 to 1/0 hooks is an ideal set up for this venue with a set of feathers or the equivalent to hand during summer if mackerel are in the vicinity. Long casting is not important and often a bait fished amongst the stanchions will score.

Some of the plaice can nudge the 3lb (1.4kg) mark.

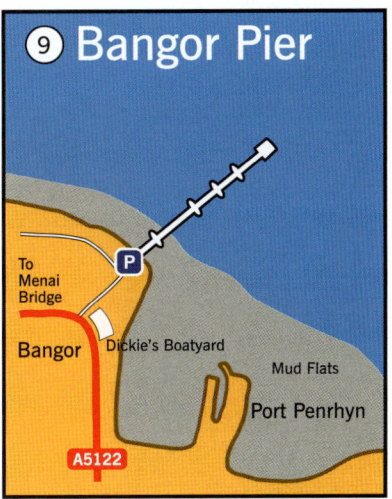

⑨ Bangor Pier

O.S. Map Sheet No. 115
Admiralty Chart No. 1464
High water: Liverpool −0hr 25
Access: 1 Comfort: 1
(See ratings at foot of page 7)

💷 CHARGES

There is a charge for fishing from the pier. In 2006 the cost is:
ADULTS £2 per session
JUNIOR £1 per session.
Night sessions by prior arrangement with the pier master (01248 354608) at £12 per group up to 10 anglers.

PWLLFANOGL, Anglesey

Quiet in winter but great variety throughout the summer

Pwllfanogl lies on the northern shore of the Menai Strait to the west of the Britannia Bridge. The length is thickly wooded just above the high water mark and as a result is unfishable over the top of the tide on all but the smallest neaps. The beach itself is comprised of weed, slate and stones falling away into a good depth of water.

How to get There

Immediately after crossing on to Anglesey via the Britannia Road/Rail Bridge take the Llanfair PG turning off the A55 Expressway. Follow this for half a mile before turning left on to the A4080, signposted to Brynsiencyn. The road leading down to the shore is a few hundred yards further along on the left and is slightly concealed. The mark runs from the small parking area at the end of this road to Plas Newydd House which is about a mile to the south west.

What & When

Results during the first few months of the year are poor with just small codling and whiting featuring in catches. The first major crab moult of the year brings an improvement in sport as dogfish, flats and a few good-sized codling arrive to feed. Most are around the 12 inch (30 cm) mark but a few better fish

A Pwllfanogl codling makes this angler smile.

Shore Marks

reaching up to 2lb (0.9kg) can be expected. As the summer progresses wrasse start to show on the patches of rough ground with the odd conger always a possibility after dark. Black bream are taken during August but considering the quantities boated by dinghies fishing well within casting range, the numbers actually beached are quite small. Triggerfish can also put in an appearance during August and September when sea temperatures are at their highest. The majority fall to peeler crab with some of the better specimens nudging the 2lb - 0.9kg mark. Autumn is the most productive time of year as an influx of codling swells the numbers of residents that, after a summer of rich feeding, have reached an acceptable size. Fish in the 1lb 8oz to 2lb 8oz (0.7 to 1.1kg) range are the average with better fish sometimes showing. Whiting, dabs and a few plaice can also be expected as well as the usual dogfish. Usually by December most of the sport will have tailed off although some years have witnessed a few codling staying on right through to early in January.

How to Catch Them

Aim to start about 3 hours after the high water at Liverpool which will give you an hour of tide running before the slack water. The slack water period and first of the flood seems most productive for all species except the codling which prefer the mid tide period when the run is at its strongest. The channel is at its deepest about 100 yards out from the low water mark and this is usually the best distance for codling. Shorter casts into the patches of rough will yield catches of ballan wrasse, conger and black bream.

BAIT

Crab is essential during the summer and into early autumn with lugworm, mussel and sandeel increasingly more effective as the year progresses.

TACKLE

Tides can be fairly strong on the springs and during the main run it can become difficult to hold the bottom but neaps aren't such a problem and a 6oz (170g) grip lead will hold. A decent cast will find relatively clear ground but expect tackle losses as you hit rocky ledges on the retrieve.

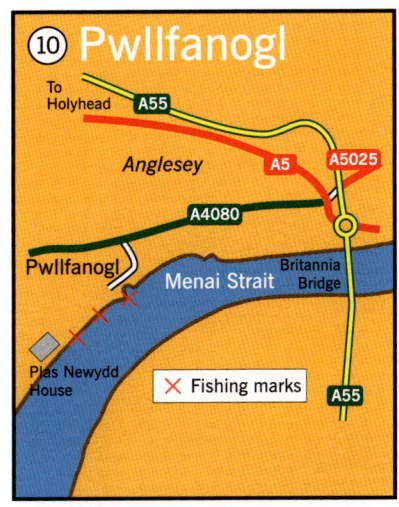

10 Pwllfanogl

O.S. Map Sheet No. 114
Admiralty Chart No. 1464
High water: Liverpool −0hr 30
Beach: Access: 2 Comfort: 3
Plas Newydd: Access: 3 Comfort: 2
(See ratings at foot of page 7)

STAR CATCH

Graham Land from nearby Llandudno took cod of 11lb 2oz (5.0kg) and 11lb 11oz (5.3kg) during a session in November 1983.

TY CROES, Anglesey

A very popular venue but often with extreme sea conditions

Ty Croes is between Rhosneigr and Aberffraw on the west of Anglesey. Fishing is from rock platforms into 20 to 40 feet (6 to 12m) of water. The sea bed is mainly sand giving way to rougher ground and kelp at the base of the rocks.

How to Get There

From junction 5 on the A55 Expressway take the A4080 towards Aberffraw before turning right about half a mile past Porth Trecastell (Cable Bay). Follow this road for about a mile then park on the right just before the entrance to the motor circuit. From here it is a comfortable 10 minute walk through the old army camp gates to the fishing marks.

What & When

January to March sees whiting in the 8 to 12oz (0.2 to 0.3kg) range, dabs, small codling and dogfish making up the bulk of catches. Spotted and thornback ray frequently appear in catches during this period and it is not unheard of for a lucky angler who times it right to land over a dozen rays in a session.

This early part of the year usually offers the better specimens with spotted ray to 4lb 8oz (2.0kg) and thornback to 14lb (6.3kg) a possibility. Better sized cod show on occasion with fish in excess of 9lb (4.0kg) landed during the last few years. Smoothhound and bull huss appear in catches from the end of May with the base of the rock edges providing food and shelter for ballan wrasse. Small cuckoo, spotted, thornback and small eyed ray can be plentiful during the summer months with grey gurnard, whiting, dabs and mackerel and dogfish bulking up the catch. As the weather cools some of the species move off leaving whiting, dabs, thornback ray, dogfish and small codling as the main winter targets. Catches can sometimes be overwhelmed by dogfish, especially in the summer months, so be prepared for some frustrating sessions.

How to Catch Them

During settled conditions it is possible to fish neap tides right over the high water period from the lower rock ledges which are more comfortable and give easier access to the water when landing fish. However, spring tides and unsettled sea conditions demand

Shore Marks

that the higher ledges be fished which owing to the nature of the rock formation tend to be more uncomfortable but safer. Aim to fish 3 hours either side of low water as this is usually the more productive period and offers the best chance of reaching the lower ledges. This venue is unfishable in winds over force 4 from the southeast round to north.

A good small-eyed ray makes it all worthwhile

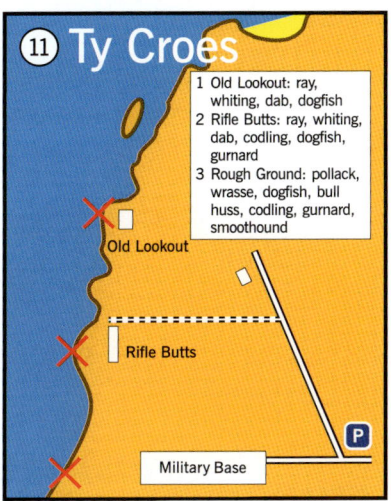

11 Ty Croes

1 Old Lookout: ray, whiting, dab, dogfish
2 Rifle Butts: ray, whiting, dab, codling, dogfish, gurnard
3 Rough Ground: pollack, wrasse, dogfish, bull huss, codling, gurnard, smoothound

Old Lookout
Rifle Butts
Military Base

TACKLE

A 2-up hook rig armed with size 1/0 strong Aberdeen style hooks like the Kamasan B940 or Mustad 79515 are ideal for the smaller fish while maximising the chances of landing larger fish. For the rays use an Up and Down rig with a 1/0 and 3/0 fished pennel style to allow for the use of larger baits. For two hours either side of the high water period on spring tides it can be difficult to hold bottom even with 6oz (170g) grip leads although the run is easier down to low and for the first 3 hours of the flood. The run on the smaller neap tides

O.S. Map Sheet No. 114
Admiralty Chart No. 1970
High water: Liverpool −1hr 30
Access: 4 Comfort: 4
(See ratings at foot of page 7)

⚠ SAFETY ANGLE

Obviously take care in an onshore wind but beware also on calm days because large groundswells can surge up the rocks and catch the unwary. South easterly winds during the mid-flood are particularly bad as they oppose the main run creating big swells. This area has claimed the lives of at least six anglers in recent years so don't underestimate the risk.

does not cause much of a problem at any stage of the tide.

BAIT

Sandeel, especially the larger ones, make ideal baits for all the rays with the smaller eels excellent for whiting, dogfish, gurnard and mackerel. Lugworm will account for the flats and codling while peeler crab scores best for smoothhound.

CABLE BAY / PORTH TRECASTELL, Anglesey

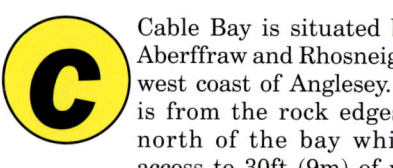

Very exposed but can offer exceptional fishing from the rocks

Cable Bay is situated between Aberffraw and Rhosneigr on the west coast of Anglesey. Fishing is from the rock edges to the north of the bay which give access to 30ft (9m) of water to a moderate cast. The sea bed is mainly clean although rock extends out for a short distance immediately below the fishing platforms and becomes extensive beyond the point at the end of the bay.

How to get There

Take junction 5 off the A55 Expressway onto the A4080 and follow the signs for Aberffraw. The car park for Cable Bay is a couple of miles before Aberffraw and is easily seen from the road. The fishing platforms are 10 minutes walk from the car park.

What & When

Whiting and dabs provide the bulk of sport from January through to March with decent codling showing when the water is coloured. Spotted ray to 4lb (1.8kg) and thornback will show when the sea settles after a blow although the average size is around the 5lb (2.25kg) mark larger fish in excess of 10lb (4.5kg) are reported every year. Dogfish dominate catches throughout spring and summer but when they are absent sport can be exceptional with spotted and small eyed rays, smoothhound, gurnard and huss likely to appear in catches. By the end of September dogfish, dabs and whiting dominate catches with thornback and spotted ray showing from time to time. Codling in the 1lb 8oz to 3lb (0.7 to 1.35kg) range may also show but as in spring, usually after a blow of wind.

How to Catch Them

Three hours either side of the low water period is generally accepted as the most productive time and also allows access to the lower ledges during calm conditions. Distance casting isn't essential but can have the edge over those fishing at short range.

BAIT

Sandeel is by far the top bait for the majority of species apart from dabs, smoothhound and codling which prefer crab and lug.

Shore Marks

The author with a spotted ray taken at Porth Trecastell

O.S. Map Sheet No. 114
Admiralty Chart No. 1970
High water: Liverpool −1hr 20
Access: 4 Comfort: 4
(See ratings at foot of page 7)

The nearest bait beds are located at Valley and Rhosneigr where lug is plentiful. Crab and ragworm can be collected from the nearby Menai Strait but as the low water period is the prime time for fishing these marks, it is advisable to bring a selection of bait with you.

TACKLE
1-up 1-down rigs work well for the smaller species with a clipped down single hook rig coupled with a larger bait working best for the rays, smoothhound and codling. There is a fairly strong tidal run on the bigger springs and although it is possible to use a plain lead on the smaller tides, a breakaway will offer better control and contact with the terminal tackle when fishing from the higher ledges.

❗ SAFETY ANGLE

A very exposed mark to be fished with caution in any wind more than force 3 from the south through to west. Even in calm conditions beware of the groundswell that builds up during mid-flood

PORTH DAFARCH, Holy Island

Very exposed but can offer exceptional fishing from the rocks

ituated on Holy Island, Anglesey, Porth Dafarch has a number of fairly comfortable rock ledges but it does require a short, steep climb to reach them. The sea bed is mainly of sand with rock running out for several yards from the base of the fishing platforms. There are a couple of platforms to the west of the bay that can be fished over high water. The most popular, known locally as Mackerel Rock, is about a 15 minute walk from the car park adjacent to the bay. The sea bed in this area is sand and rocky patches.

How to Get There

Take junction 3 off the A55 Expressway and follow the A5 towards Valley. At Valley take the B4545 and head towards Trearrdur Bay.

John Waugh with a 9lb (4.1kg) February cod

Shore Marks

Pass through Trearddur Bay then take the first left towards Porth Dafarch which is approximately two miles further on. To access the promontories to the east of the bay, park in the lay by adjacent to the small beach and walk along the cliff path. The Mackerel Rock area is reached by taking the road half a mile past the bay which leads to a small car park.

What & When

Porth Dafarch is sheltered from winds from the north west through to south east but can be unfishable in anything above force 5 from the south to west. The area is heavily fished in summer and produces wrasse, pollack, mackerel, flats, gurnard, spotted and small eyed rays. After dark the place can come alive with dogfish but this becomes less of a problem as winter closes in. Winter sees less angling activity although sport can be excellent. Coalfish are the main species at around the 1 or 2lb (0.45 to 0.9kg) mark with occasional larger fish to 4lb (1.8kg). Codling can also be expected especially after a strong wind has put some colour into the water. Although the average size is around the 2lb (0.9kg) mark larger fish several times heavier are caught, especially during January and February. Along with the coalfish and codling other species likely to be taken include dogfish, dabs, small plaice and whiting. Dogfish can be prolific during the spring but the area is better known for the early showing of mackerel, usually during mid-April.

How to Catch Them

The most productive time to fish is 3 hours either side of low water which also allows access to the lower ledges. To the east of the bay the tide run is light but can be strong to the west of the bay and in particular in front of Mackerel Rock.

TACKLE

Conventional beach gear with 18lb (8kg) BS main line will cope with the cleaner ground but 25lb (11.5kg) BS is advisable when fishing the rougher areas. A range of breakaway leads from 4 to 6oz (110 to 170g) should be enough to cope with the tide run on all but the largest springs.

BAIT

Lug, rag and sandeel are all productive but sometimes fresh or frozen crab will have the edge, especially during the winter months.

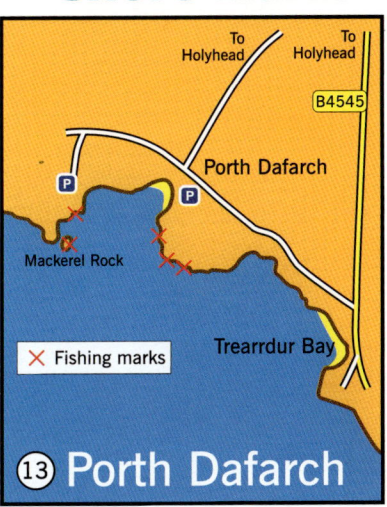

O.S. Map Sheet No. 114
Admiralty Chart No. 1970
High water: Liverpool −0hr 50
Access: 4 Comfort: 4
(See ratings at foot of page 7)

STAR CATCH

R. Williams from Holyhead holds the Welsh record for mackerel with a 4lb 5oz (1.95kg fish caught here in July 1990.

HOLYHEAD BREAKWATER, Holy Is

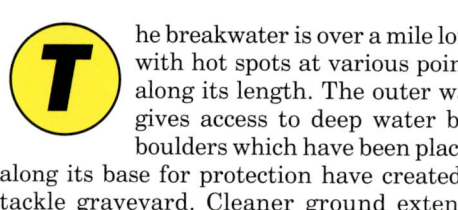

A mile out to sea expect a mixed catch

The breakwater is over a mile long with hot spots at various points along its length. The outer wall gives access to deep water but boulders which have been placed along its base for protection have created a tackle graveyard. Cleaner ground extends from the end of the breakwater right along the inside wall

How to Get There

Take the A55 onto Anglesey following signs for Holyhead. This road takes you through the town itself, past the Ferry Terminal and on to the coast road that skirts the new harbour. Take a left just before the Boat House Hotel and then turn right at the gate through the Stena yard to the start of the breakwater. There is plenty of parking space by the gate.

What & When

The outer wall produces mixed bags throughout the year but the main species are wrasse, three-bearded rockling, dogfish and large pout. Pollack also show in good numbers and although the average size is only around the 1lb 8oz to 2lb (0.7 to 0.9kg) mark bigger fish 10lb+ (4.5kg+ are sometimes landed but more are lost due to a lack of a drop net and the very heavy ground. Sport in the inner harbour cannot compare with the outer wall but dabs, dogfish, conger, mostly small but some up to 20lb (9.0kg), and whiting offer a less strenuous session. The end of the breakwater produces dogfish and at times during the early summer smoothhound with a run of bull huss during September and October. The best sport is during the winter months when the codling shoals move in. These are mainly in the 1 to 3lb (0.45 to 1.35kg) range but larger fish of 5 to 10lb (2.25 to 4.5kg) do show on occasion. Large bags of whiting can also be taken with some fish topping 1lb 12oz (0.8kg). Other species caught during the year include mackerel, mullet, ling and the occasional ray.

How to Catch Them

Fish the outside wall from mid tide until a couple of hours after high water. The end section is best fished over the whole of the ebb using the tide to move the tackle through an arc thereby covering more of the seabed.

Shore Marks

Easy parking at the start of the Breakwater and level access right to the far end makes Holyhead Breakwater an ideal location for anglers who might have difficulty reaching some other fishing marks.

⑭ **Holyhead Breakwater**

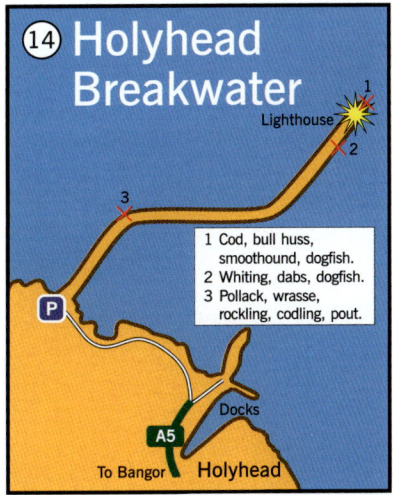

1. Cod, bull huss, smoothhound, dogfish.
2. Whiting, dabs, dogfish.
3. Pollack, wrasse, rockling, codling, pout.

BAIT
Bait requirements are straightforward, lug and mackerel in winter with crab, sandeel and lugworm preferable during summer. Large lug baits fished on the ebb when the tide screams out of the harbour are the most productive for the winter codling.

TACKLE
The outer wall demands heavy gear with 25lb (12kg) main line to a rotten bottom a must. When fishing the end section a standard beachcasting will suffice but a range of breakaway leads from 5 to 8oz (140 to 225g) are needed to counter the tidal flow.

A variety of colourful wrasse populate the boulders at the base of at the Breakwater

O.S. Map Sheet No. 114
Admiralty Chart No. 1970
High water: Liverpool –0hr 50
Gate open: Access: 2 Comfort: 1
Gate closed: Access: 3 Comfort: 1
(See ratings at foot of page 7)

STAR CATCH
A memorable catch from Holyhead breakwater was a tadpole fish of 1lb 2oz (0.5kg) caught by Mike Robinson in October 1985.

BULL BAY, Anglesey

Conger can be expected after dark

The rock edges at Bull Bay are on the north coast of Anglesey between Amlwch and Cemaes Bay. The venue offers deep water at all stages of the tide but due to the formation of the rock there are only a few comfortable fishing platforms. The sea bed is rough at close range although small areas of cleaner ground can be found at distance. This venue faces north so it is sheltered from the prevailing south westerly winds but even so care must be taken, especially on spring tides, during the middle flood when surges can wash up the rocks.

How to Get There

After crossing onto Anglesey take the A5025 at the Four Crosses Hotel and follow signs for Amlwch which is about 17 miles from the bridge. Leave the A5025 at the Bull Bay turn off 2 miles west of Amlwch and park either adjacent to or just past the Bull Bay Hotel. The village is popular with holiday makers during the summer months and as a result parking space can be limited.

What & When

During the early part of the year the mark can fish well for pollack, whiting and dogfish on sandeel with worm baits attracting plenty of small codling. Wrasse up to 3lb (1.35kg) can be expected during the summer along with pollack, mackerel and herring falling to artificial lures. The hours of darkness can produce conger in the 8 to 15lb (3.6 to 6.8kg) bracket along with three-bearded rockling and dogfish. Good bags of whiting are often taken over the cleaner patches during the autumn with codling also a possibility. Other species that appear less frequently include tadpole fish, coalfish, dabs, ling and bull huss.

How to Catch Them

Tides in this area can be fairly strong, especially on the flood, and it is essential to use grip leads when fishing at distance. At shorter range the sea bed can be snaggy so a change to a "rotten bottom" will often be required.

Shore Marks

TACKLE
Pollack, mackerel and herring will fall to artificial lures but float fishing ragworm can also be a successful method, especially for pollack.

BAIT
Early in the year worm baits coupled with sandeel will account for the majority of available species with the exception of conger that favour mackerel or better still a freshly caught whiting or poor cod. The same baits will fish well during the summer although peeler crab will score heavily especially for wrasse.

Typical night-time winter conger.

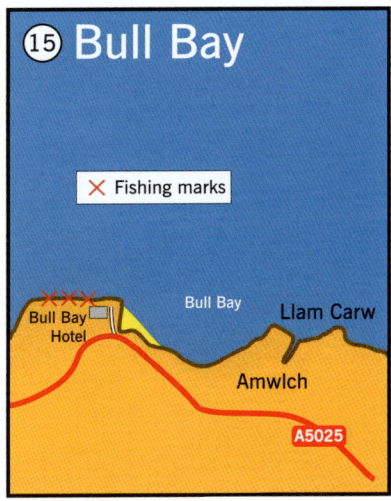

O.S. Map Sheet No. 114
Admiralty Chart No. 1977
High water: Liverpool −0hr 35
Access: 4   Comfort: 5
(See ratings at foot of page 7)

✺ TOP TIP

The area is well served by camp sites, caravan parks and guest houses. For further information contact the local Tourist Information Centre on 01407 762622

LLAM CARW, Anglesey

A favourite winter venue well sheltered and very productive

Llam Carw is a rocky stretch of coastline on the northern coast of Anglesey and lies between Amlwch and Point Lynas. Fishing is from rock platforms into 40 to 60ft (12 to 18m) of water onto mainly sand although there are patches of foul ground in front of some of the marks.

How to Get There

Cross onto Anglesey and follow the A5025 through Benllech before turning off at the roundabout just before Amlwch. Follow signs to Amlwch Port and where the road splits just before the port take the top road which leads past the harbour to a car park adjacent to a grey building. To reach the more productive rock ledges go through the gate and over a stile following the footpath towards Eilean Bay until you reach a wall which marks the start of the better spots.

What & When

Look for a medium sized tide and aim to fish a couple of hours either side of low water which given calm conditions will allow access to the lower ledges and small islets that offer more comfortable fishing conditions. Sport during the first three months of the year can be very good. This and the excellent shelter from the prevailing south to westerly winds makes Llam Carw a very popular winter venue. Whiting in the 8 to 12oz (0.22 to 0.34kg) range are the dominant species with specimens up to 1lb 12oz (0.8kg) taken every year. Codling in the 1lb 8oz to 3lb (0.675 to 1.35kg) range can also show along with dabs, dogfish, and poor cod. Pollack and wrasse can be expected over the rougher ground as the year progresses and make up the bulk of the summer catches, along with dabs, dogfish, mackerel and occasionally herring. Sessions after dark will produce three-bearded rockling and reasonable chances of conger in the 5 to 15lb (2.25 to 6.75kg) range for those who specialise. Whiting start to increase in numbers during September with codling showing to a greater or lesser extent depending on the quality of that year's inshore migration. These two species together with dabs, dogfish, poor cod and pollack will offer the majority of the sport to the turn of the year.

Shore Marks

How to Catch Them

BAIT

In common with many of the rock marks in North Wales, sandeel tends to be the more productive bait taking the majority of the species available. Lug and crab are possibly better than sandeel for codling and in particular, wrasse.

TACKLE

A 2 up rig fished at a distance of between 60 and 100 yards (55 to 90m will suffice on most occasions but there are times when a longer cast will be more productive so it pays to vary your distance. Grip leads in the 150 to 170g) range will be adequate for all but the worst of the tide run.

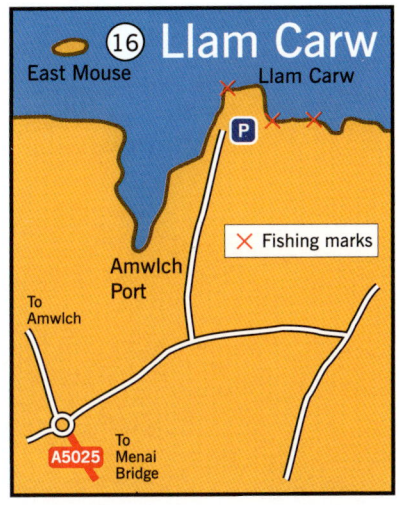

O.S. Map Sheet No. 114
Admiralty Chart No. 1970
LOW water: Liverpool −0hr 40
Access: 4 Comfort: 4&5
(See ratings at foot of page 7)

✻ TOP TIP

The tidal run on the medium to spring tides can be fierce during the middle of the flood and ebb but the best of the fishing is a couple of hours either side of low water so it is a problem that should rarely be experienced

Llam Carw is good in summer too, especially for pollack (above) and wrasse.

POINT LYNAS, Anglesey

A three-sided venue but not all sides are easily fishable

Point Lynas is a major Anglesey landmark with a lighthouse located a couple of miles east of the fishing port of Amlwch on the north coast. The rock ledges can be reached via a fairly gentle climb and although all three sides of the promontory can be fished the front, beneath the light house, suffers the worst of the tide. The bottom can be very rough in places but conversely there are also large patches of sand, especially on the Llaneilian Bay side of the point and towards Freshwater Bay.

How to Get There

After crossing onto Anglesey follow the A5025 for approximately 15 miles, passing through Pentraeth and Benllech, before turning right into the village of Penysarn. Turn right just past the grocer's before taking a sharp left at the next junction. Follow this road for a mile then turn right at the T junction next to the telephone box. Follow the road through Llaneilian Bay and park at the main gate that leads to the lighthouse. There is a charge for parking during the main summer months.

What & When

During the early part of the year there is very little activity although results can be very good. Whiting can be prolific over the cleaner patches with specimens nudging the 1lb 8oz (0.675kg) mark a possibility, especially during January and February. Dabs and dogfish also feature with rockling, pollack in the 1lb to 2lb (0.45 to 0.9kg) range and a few conger over the rough ground. Codling will also appear in catches but tend not to be prolific. The deep water also attracts small ling. Wrasse and pollack over the rougher ground dominate daytime catches during the summer and after dark conger up to 15lb (6.75kg), dogfish, rockling and the odd bull huss. The sandier areas can produce dabs, small whiting and dogfish. Summer anglers can also expect shoals of mackerel to show on occasion with herring also taken from time to time. As October approaches better sized whiting move inshore and together with dabs, dogfish, pollack and poor cod are the main targets for the rest of the winter. Other species that may be encountered during the year include coalfish, plaice, tadpole fish and mullet.

Shore Marks

How to Catch Them

The tide run inside Llaneilian Bay is light but in front of the light house the current during the middle flood and ebb is such that on spring tides it can become impossible to hold bottom and due to the snaggy ground tackle losses can be excessive. As a result slack water periods over high and low water are the more productive times to fish. South towards Freshwater Bay the tide run on spring tides coupled with the depth of water can make ledgering difficult during the height of the run but a 6oz (170g) grip lead fished "uptide" should hold on this predominantly sandy area.

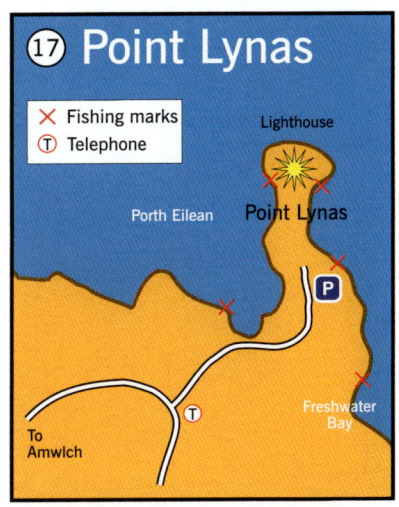

Conger can be anticipated during the winter months.

BAIT
Crab, worm and mackerel are all productive but the most consistent bait is sandeel.

TACKLE
Keep the end tackle simple over the rough ground and use just a single hook rig with a rotten bottom to reduce fish and tackle losses. Float fishing is a great method of enjoying sport with the many small pollack which tend to shoal in the cove to the left of the lighthouse.

O.S. Map Sheet No. 114
Admiralty Chart No. 1977
LOW water: Liverpool –0hr 30
Access: 4 Comfort: 4
(See ratings at foot of page 7)

STAR CATCH

Point Lynas was the venue for the Welsh record sunfish at 15lb 7oz (7.0kg), caught in July 1995 by M. Bickerton of Abergele.

WHITEBEACH, Anglesey

The old quarry workings have left rock platforms ideal for angling

On the south east corner of Anglesey the rock platforms at Whitebeach were hewn from the granite during the early part of the twentieth century when the area was extensively quarried. The paths down to the marks are gently sloping but can be slippery especially after periods of heavy rain. The seabed in front of the fishing platforms is comprised of sand and shell with patches of rock close in and within the bays. The ledges themselves are terraced and so access to the water's edge is easy when conditions allow.

East facing and with cliffs behind, the rock edges are well protected from the prevailing west to south west winds and it is only when the wind is over a force 4 from the north west to east quadrant that conditions become too difficult to fish safely.

How to Get There

Immediately after crossing onto Anglesey via the Britannia Bridge take the first exit off the Expressway and turn right towards Menai Bridge. Follow the A545 / B5109 through Beaumaris and on to Llangoed. At Llangoed take the left turn and follow this road towards Llandonna for about 1 mile before taking the right hand fork just past the telephone box. The next road on the left, identified by a No Through Road sign, will take you down to the cliff tops overlooking the rock edges. There is a small turning area and parking at the end of the track.

What & When

Dogfish start to show at the beginning of March increasing in numbers as Spring progresses. Small whiting in the 6 to 10oz (0.17 to 0.25kg) range are also in attendance especially on the larger tides when jetsam from the nearby estuaries colours the water and attracts the fish closer to shore. Dabs, small codling, herring and an occasional plaice can also be expected. Thornback sometimes move within casting range with several 10lb+ (4.5kg+) fish recorded from the area. Late spring to early summer sees wrasse and pollack appearing in catches with quality conger a possibility after dark. Mackerel are plentiful throughout the summer months particularly during settled spells. Other species that can be expected to show at times during the summer

Shore Marks

months are grey gurnard, smoothhound, garfish and bass. September sees the summer species replaced by dense shoals of whiting which provide excellent sport after dark. They average around the 12oz (0.3kg) mark but larger specimens to 1lb 12oz (0.8kg) are taken every year. Along with dogfish and a few dabs they provide the bulk of sport throughout the winter months with codling 1lb 4oz to 3lb (0.6 to 1.35kg) featuring to a greater or lesser extent depending on the year class.

How to Catch Them

The two more prominent ledges looking towards Puffin Island are the more popular marks but be aware that access to the further promontory via the field is now prohibited. The field in question is officially a Site of Special Scientific Interest and access is a very sensitive issue. There are other and arguably more productive ledges a 10 minute walk west of the car park towards Llandona Although there is a noticeable tidal run, especially on the ebb, a 6oz (170g) grip lead will hold bottom comfortably on tides between 7 and 9m (Liverpool) and it is only on the bigger spring tides, and then only for a short period, that this becomes difficult.

BAIT

Frozen sandeel takes some beating as an all round bait especially late and early in the season when dogs and whiting dominate catches. Codling, wrasse and flats and any smoothhound that are taken invariably fall to lug or crab.

TACKLE

A one up one down rig ledgered at a distance will account for most species with bass falling to plugs or spinners fished close

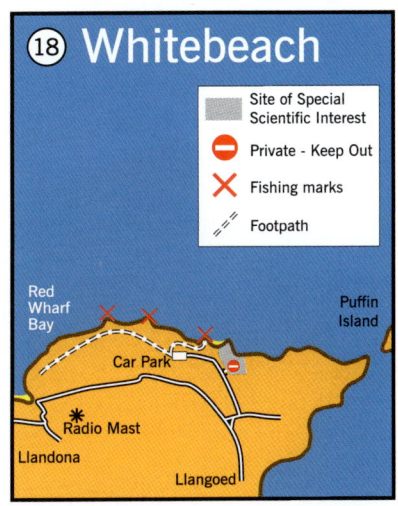

⑱ Whitebeach

- Site of Special Scientific Interest
- Private - Keep Out
- Fishing marks
- Footpath

O.S. Map Sheet Nos. 114/115
Admiralty Chart No. 1977
LOW water: Liverpool –0hr 25
Access: 4 Comfort: 4
(See ratings at foot of page 7)

in to the rock edges at dawn or dusk. The rock promontories and tidal run well suited to ground baiting and one of the most successful methods of catching the pelagic species such as mackerel and garfish is to floatfish small pieces of fish bait into a rubby dubby trail of minced fish, bran and fish oil. Sandeel and pollack are also attracted to the trail as are mullet and bass.

A very good dab from Whitebeach.

47

DEGANWY

Easy spring angling as the fish seek the peeler crabs

ituated on the northern shore of the Conwy estuary this venue stretches from the dock wall a few hundred yards east of the promenade to the old pipe at the estuary mouth just below Llandudno West Shore. The beach is shingle, stones and sand. On the sea bed this is interspersed by weed and mussel beds.

How to Get There

From the A55 Expressway take the A546 through Llandudno Junction to the roundabout following signs for Deganwy before turning left onto the promenade just after the signal box. There is plenty of parking space on the road alongside the estuary leaving just a short walk down the shingle to the waters edge.

What & When

January to March are the quietest months of the year with catches restricted to rockling and a few flounder. The end of March sees flounder returning to the estuary after spawning and increasing in numbers to peak in May and early June. The average size is around the 12oz (0.3kg) mark but every season sees many specimens between 1lb 8oz and 2lb 6oz (0.45 and 1.1kg) taken. Codling can also be expected during this period as they move into the river to feed heavily on crab and although many fish fail to top the 1lb (0.45kg) mark there are usually better sized fish to 3lb (1.35kg) amongst the shoals. The venue also produces good numbers of school bass and very few years go by without a 10lb+ (4.5kg+) fish landed. Codling tend to leave the estuary after the main crab moult and the numbers of flounder, eels and bass also decline. This results in a lean period during July and August. Sport improves during September and October and with codling in the 1lb 4oz to 2lb 8oz (0.6 to 1.1kg) range returning to the estuary and producing some of the best catches of the year. Results can hold up into November but an influx of melted snow water from the mountains any time after this can bring about a premature end to the season as the colder water drives food and consequently fish out of the river.

••• Shore Marks •••

Deganwy is well known for its quality flounder.

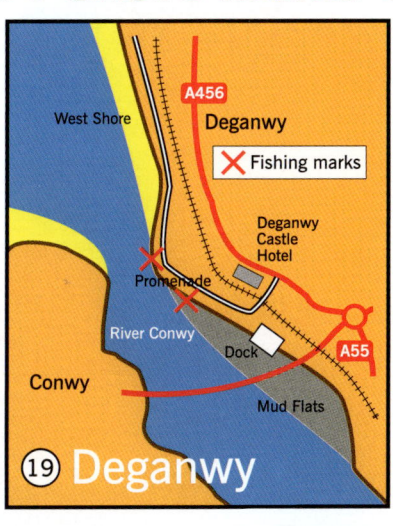

HOW TO CATCH THEM

The venue produces best on the last 3 hours of the ebb and first 2 of the flood. As a rule of thumb the flounder tend to feed better over the slack water period with the codling and bass favouring the run. However, a very short cast during the worst of the tide can often find fish feeding in the shallows as they take advantage of the comparatively slacker water.

BAIT

Ragworm and lugworm will take fish early and late in the year when the sea temperatures are cooler and crab less active but once things warm up then peeler crab is the main bait.

TACKLE

As distance casting is unnecessary due to the narrowness of the channel, a two-hook rig loaded with size 1/0 hooks and large baits will account for the better sized fish scaling down to size 2 when fish are scarce. Breakaway leads in the 6 to 7oz (150g to 170g) range will hold bottom during the worst of the tide run but do not be afraid, if the situation allows, to fish light as a moving bait can be very productive.

O.S. Map Sheet No. 115
Admiralty Chart No. 1977
High water: Liverpool −0hr 30
Access: 2 Comfort: 2
(See ratings at foot of page 7)

★ STAR CATCH

Mick Flynn from Anglesey won a match at Deganwy in May 1999, helped by flounder of 2lb 15½oz and 2lb 14½oz, (about 1.3kg) each caught on the same cast.

LLANDUDNO PIER

Fish from the end of a fine Victorian pier

Lying at the foot of the Great Orme on the north coast of Wales the seaside town of Llandudno boasts one of the finest Victorian piers left in the country. It is well sheltered from the south and west but exposed to winds from the north but as long as it is not too strong an onshore blow can often increase catches. A wide range of accommodation is available in the town, contact the Welsh Tourist Board Office - see Directory section for details.

How to Get There

From the A55 Expressway take the A470 turn off and follow the signs for Llandudno. The pier is located at the western end of the promenade in the lee of the Great Orme. The pier has two entrances which dictate parking preferences. If the top gate is used, use the Pay and Display car park just past the Grand Hotel. For the lower gate it's best to park on the promenade itself. Obviously, as Llandudno is a seaside resort parking space can be at something of a premium during the main holiday periods and at weekends.

What & When

The main body of the pier used to boast some excellent and comfortable fishing but due to health and safety reasons fishing is now confined to the concrete platform at the pier head. Due to the limited space available it can be somewhat cramped at times especially during the summer so take care when casting. The platform which is accessed via a ramp gives access to deep water at all stages of the tide but a couple of hours either side of the low water is generally regarded as the more productive period. Dabs, small whiting and dogs make up the bulk of catches early in the year. Thornback ray can also appear at this time but more arrive in May and June when they favour a good sized offering of peeler or soft crab. Later in the month and into July the same bait will find smoothhound of 4 to 8lb (1.8 to 3.6kg). The main summer months offer exciting sport for those using lures when shoals of mackerel come within casting range while float fished baits close to the platform supports can produce mullet, scad, mackerel, small pollack and coalfish. Bottom fished baits will find dabs, wrasse, black bream, gurnard

Shore Marks

> Llandudno Pier is smooth and flat for most of its length and there is ample parking space available nearby, making it an excellent choice for those who need easy access to comfortable fishing.

and dogs with conger falling to large fish baits offered at the base of the platform. Catches during the autumn and early winter consist of pout, dabs, coalfish, whiting, rockling and dogs. Codling average around the 2lb (1kg) mark with the occasional larger fish into double figures so it can be worthwhile bringing a drop net.

How to Catch Them

Due to the sheltering effect of the Great Orme the tides are fairly gentle although on springs a 5oz (140g) breakaway lead may be necessary. However, if there is space, a rolling lead will outfish a fixed one.

TACKLE
Conventional beach outfit with a 2 hook rig is the norm at this venue although if targeting the rays and smoothhound go down to a single larger hook and increase bait size. A spinning rod with light main line will allow the smaller species that congregate amongst the stanchions to show their fighting abilities whilst also ideal for any mullet that might be around.

BAIT
Sandeel, lug and ragworm are successful throughout the year with peeler crab essential for spring codling and smoothhound. Mackerel will pick up conger beneath the pier and was the bait that tempted a 17lb (7.7kg) bass in 1998. A wide selection of bait is available from Rays Tackle and Bait at the entrance to the pier. Hire rods are also available. The shop is open 7 days a week from 0800 to 1700hrs in the winter and closes at 2000hrs during the summer. Tel 01492877678.

There may be restrictions on opening times during winter so it would be advisable to check before travelling between October and March. There has been the suggestion of introducing a permit system to replace the charges shown (right) but at the time of going to print no decision had been made.

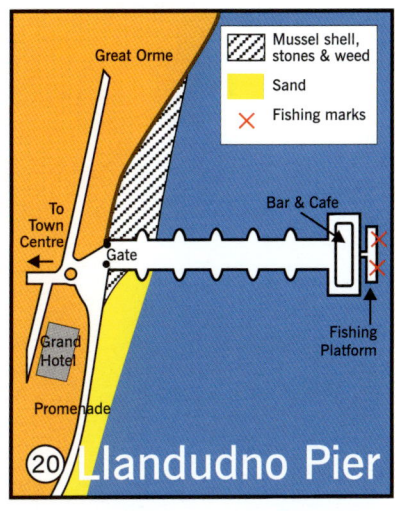

O.S. Map Sheet No. 115 or 116
Admiralty Chart No. 1977
High water: Liverpool –0hr 30
Access: 1 Comfort: 1
(See ratings at foot of page 7)

£ CHARGES

Collected by a warden:

08.00 to 12.00 £1.50
12.00 to 16.00 £1.50
16.00 to 20.00 £1.50
22.00 to 02.00 £2.00
ALL DAY £4.00

(2007 prices)

LLANDUDNO NORTH SHORE

A top match fishing venue

The length of shingle stretching between the Great and Little Ormes at Llandudno may not be one of the most productive beaches in North Wales but in autumn its popularity increases as it hosts a number of matches. The shingle bank stretches beyond the low water mark on neap tides but on springs a band of sand is exposed especially towards the pier where the beach is slightly shallower. The bottom is clean apart from the area behind the cottages at the Little Orme end but this section is usually out of bounds so the advantage offered by the rough terrain is lost. Protected by the North Wales landmass and the Ormes, the beach is well sheltered from all winds except northerlies.

How to Get There

Leave the A55 at the A470 then follow the signs to Llandudno. The road follows the shoreline at the eastern end of the match length with the usual booking on site located halfway along the promenade at the Paddling Pool. Parking is available the full length of the promenade.

What & When

Catches during the first few months of the year are disappointing with usually just small whiting and rockling being taken. April sees an improvement as dogfish and a few flounder and plaice move within casting distance. Codling can also show at this period in the year but they are usually small unless a good sea is running which tends to attract the better fish to 3lb (1.35kg) inshore. During July and August a settled spell of weather coupled with an evening high water will often attract shoals of mackerel into the bay which along with small whiting, dogfish and the occasional flatfish dominate catches throughout the main holiday period. Bass will sometimes be taken over the rough ground behind the houses during this period but the best catches are taken in September and early October and then only if a good surf is running. From October until the end of December whiting and dogfish are the main target species with dabs, five-bearded rockling, flounder and a few sizeable codling featuring in catches on occasion.

● ● ● ● ● ● ● ● ● Shore Marks ● ● ●

Plaice like this can help win matches.

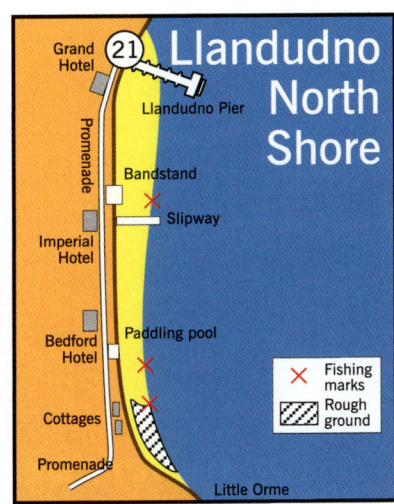

O.S. Map Sheet No. 115 or 116
Admiralty Chart No. 1978
High water: Liverpool −0hr 25
Access: 2 Comfort: 2
(See ratings at foot of page 7)

How to Catch Them

Because of the sheltering effect of the two headlands at either end of the beach the tide run is minimal. However over the high water period on springs there can be a fair run especially for those hitting baits a good distance.

BAIT

Sandeel is by far the more productive bait for the dogfish and whiting with black lug and ragworm picking off the flats. Codling prefer peeler crab and to a lesser degree lugworm with the better bass falling to soft or peeler crab and whole calamari squid .

TACKLE

Apart from flatfish, and when a surf is running, bass and codling, most of the better catches are taken at long range after dark. A two- or three-hook paternoster rig clipped down for distance with 1/0 to 2/0 hooks at the business end is ideal for dogs and whiting while scaling down the number but increasing the size of hook and bait when a surf is running and increasing the chance of codling and bass.

53

TAN Y LAN

An anglers beach with few attractions for tourists but plenty of fish all year round

ituated at the eastern end of Colwyn Bay, the beach at Tan y Lan at Old Colwyn stretches from the end of the promenade road to Penmaen Head. The section from the end of the promenade to the headland is cut by a number of groynes. For the most part the beach is clean but there are patches of stone and small boulders beyond the low water mark towards the headland.

How to Get There

Take the Old Colwyn turn off at junction 22 of the A55 Expressway and turn right towards the sea front. At the junction with the promenade turn right and follow the road a few hundred yards before parking at the end of the promenade just before the railway bridge. The headland is at the far end of the section, about a 10 minute walk along the cycle path.

What & When

From January through to March good bags of whiting averaging around the 12oz (0.3kg) mark with a fair proportion topping the 1lb (0.45kg) mark can be expected after dark on spring tides. Thornback can also been caught but inshore trawling during recent years has reduced their numbers. Dogfish move in during April and stay in varying numbers until the end of the year, making it a popular match venue. Bass are often taken from June to September with the better fish usually taken over low water amongst the rocks at the base of Penmaen Head. Whiting return in September and are at their peak during October and November. Codling in the 1lb to 3lb (0.45 to 1.35kg) range can also show around this time but their numbers tend to be unpredictable with some years boasting good quantities and other years with almost none. Other species likely to make an appearance during the year are flounder, dabs and rockling.

How to Catch Them

There is very little tide run on this beach but even so larger spring tides are generally more productive than neaps. Over high water it is possible to fish from the narrow parapet which runs as far as the archway with the promenade frontage giving way to large

Shore Marks

㉒ Tan y Lan

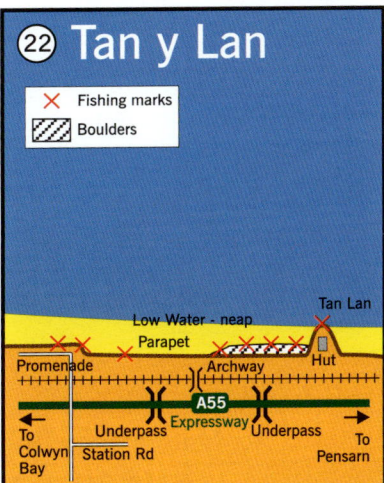

Tan Llan in late autumn is the place for a big bag of whiting.

granite boulders beyond this point. On the smaller tides fishing is possible over high water from the stony foreshore at the foot of the boulders but during rough weather and over the bigger tides it has to be from the path at the top. Casting from the parapet is difficult due to the fence behind but there are a couple of places, the archway is one, where it widens out making casting easier. During autumn and winter distance casting over the low water period can often pick up codling and dogs but once the tide starts to build catches are dominated by whiting which can often be contacted within 40 or so yards orm of the rod tip. As a rule the hours of darkness are far more productive than the day.

BAIT

Mackerel strip and the local black lug, known as "sewies" are the prime baits throughout the winter months although mussel, sandeel and rag all take their fair share of fish. Peeler or large soft crab are essential for the bass that feed over the rough ground and can also produce the better bags of codling during the winter.

TACKLE

Two- or three-hook rigs score heavily with the whiting but for cod a large lug offering mounted on a single hook rig will help find that essential extra distance.

O.S. Map Sheet No. 116
Admiralty Chart No. 1978
High water: Liverpool –0hr 30
Access: 2 Comfort: 3
(See ratings at foot of page 7)

✱ TOP TIP

A moderate south westerly wind puts colour in the water and produces the best results while a fresh west to northwesterly can make the mark unfishable and during high water, dangerous.

MOSTYN

The sheltered embankment and sandbanks in the estuary allow fishing even in poor weather

This little quarry port is on the Welsh side of the Dee estuary between Flint and Prestatyn. Fishing is from a fairly comfortable stone embankment into a channel which is no more than 200m wide at low water. The bed is mainly sand and the odd stone so tackle losses are few.

Mostyn has much more than flatfish but this flounder is a fine specimen.

How to get There
From Connah's Quay take the A548 coast road through Flint, Bagillt and Greenfield before turning right just after the Post Office and opposite the Robert Davies Memorial Church Hall. There is limited parking at the end of the lane adjacent to the sea wall, to the left towards the docks and towards the Fun Ship on the right.

What & When
From January to early March the main catches are whiting, dabs and a few codling none of which are as prolific as at the end of the year but they still provide good sport. Plaice become the main target from the middle of March to July with results at their best from late April to early June. They

Shore Marks

normally average around 1lb (0.45kg) with specimens to 2lb 8oz (1.1kg) not unusual. Better sized fish put in the odd appearance with a couple of fish around the 4lb (1.8kg) mark landed in recent years. Dabs, flounder, eels and codling, some in the 1lb 8oz to 2lb 8oz (0.7 to 1.1kg) bracket, can also be expected. Results dip during the summer months but improve dramatically with the arrival of the whiting shoals from the middle of September onwards. The whiting are of a good average size and in such numbers that matches often produce 30-fish bags weighing in excess of 20lb (9.0kg). Codling in the 1lb 4oz to 2lb 8oz (0.6 to 1.1kg) range start to appear in catches at the start of October and, along with whiting and dabs, stay for the best part of the winter. A few better sized fish in the 4 to 6lb (1.8 to 2.7kg) range are sometimes taken with the best reported in recent years being fish of 17lb (7.7kg) taken during the winter of 97/98.

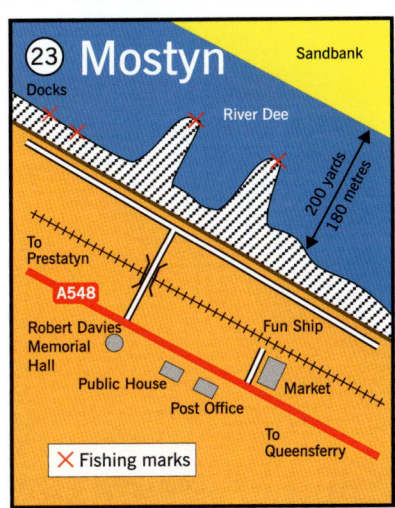

How to Catch them

To the left and right of the T junction are two spits of rock which project into the channel which are regarded by many as hotspots but in truth any point on the embankment can be good on the day. Although it is possible to fish over high water on neap tides most of the action is during the last 3 hours of the ebb and first 2 on the flood with the first and last hours of the period having the strongest run. During these periods a 6oz (170g) breakaway will be required to hold bottom but the tide eases very quickly and it is possible to fish a plain 4 to 5oz (125 to 150g) lead for most of the session

O.S. Map Sheet No. 116
Admiralty Chart No. 1978
High water: Liverpool –0hr 1
Access: 2 Comfort: 2
(See ratings at foot of page 7)

BAIT
From March through to October the premier bait is peeler crab and although fish will be taken on other baits, especially when the tide is running hard, the local crab population soon make a meal of worm and fish baits. As the sea temperature cools the crabs become less active and consequently the effectiveness of these baits increase but codling in the majority of circumstances will favour fresh peeler or soft crab.

TACKLE
A two- to three-hook rig, depending on the amount of bait available, fished above the lead works in most circumstances with hook sizes varying between size 1 and 2/0 depending on the target species and size of bait offered. Long casting is unnecessary with most fish taken at a range of between 10 and 80m.

! SAFETY ANGLE

The last ten metres of the embankment shelves very steeply into the channel and can sometimes prove hazardous when landing better sized fish or retrieving snagged tackle.

GREENFIELD

Some of the finest flatfish fishing in North Wales

Located on the western bank of the Dee Estuary between Flint and Mostyn, the beach at Greenfield offers some of the finest flatfish fishing in North Wales. Fishing is from a steeply sloping and slightly uncomfortable rocky bank into a gulley which runs along the base of the embankment. The sea bed is mostly sand and shell with any tackle losses occurring when terminal tackle is swept by into the rocks at the foot of the embankment.

How to get There

From Queensferry follow the A548 through Connah's Quay and Flint to Greenfield then turn right into Dock Road immediately before the Queens Head pub. Follow this road over the railway bridge for a quarter mile and park on the left hand side of the small harbour.

What and When

During January and February bags are made up of rockling, whiting and flounder some of which can nudge the 2lb 0.9kg) mark. Results drop off from the middle of February until the end of March when plaice, thin after spawning, move in to feed on the shellfish in the estuary. Their numbers increase during April and peak in early May. The average size of the plaice is around the 1lb (0.45kg) mark with better specimens twice that weight always possibile, especially in early summer when the fish have regained condition. Flounder and eels will also appear in catches especially from the marks to the right of the car park although usually to the detriment of numbers of plaice in your catch. The better marks for plaice are to the left of the car park towards the Fun Ship. Get there by crossing the stile and following the path (Pennant Walk) alongside the embankment.

Catches decline in mid summer but improve during the autumn when the flats are joined by whiting and the occasional codling.

How to Catch Them

Although on neap tides it is possible to fish from a couple of hours after low water until a couple of hours before the next low water and even longer in the deeper water to the south of the harbour, the best fishing is during the middle section of both the flood and ebb. On the ebb start your session a couple of hours

Shore Marks

after high water when the sandbanks are starting to uncover and end about two hours before low water when the gutter is almost dry. This also allows you to fish off the flatter section of the embankment and not the boulders. Sport will be slow at first, not helped by the strong tidal flow, but results improve as the fish start to move off the drying banks and concentrate in the gulley. On the flood start your session about an hour and a half after low water just as the gulley starts to fill. Sport can be quite frenetic for the first hour and it pays to have a spare pre-baited rig ready. Results tail off as the tide starts to cover the banks although fish will still be caught during the remainder of the flood but not usually in the same numbers. During late autumn and early winter high water slack can be very productive for whiting especially when fishing from the large boulders by the harbour entrance.

BAIT
Ragworm, lug and mussel are all good but peeler is the most successful bait. Frozen peeler is an excellent alternative especially for flats early in the season.

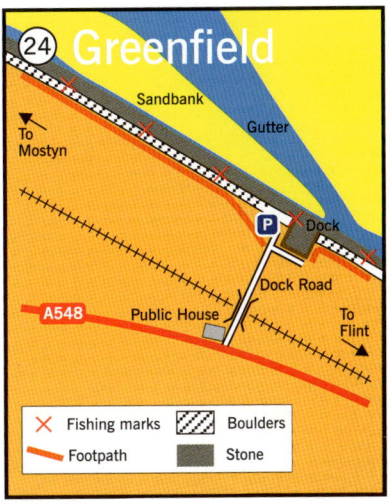

O.S Map Sheet No. 116
Admiralty Chart No. 1978
High water: Liverpool −0hr 15
Access 4 comfort 3
See ratings at foot of page 7

TACKLE
A one-up one-down rig with size 1 or 2 Aberdeen hooks fished at short range is the accepted method. A 4oz (100g) plain lead will hold bottom for most of the time but grip leads are needed when the tide is running.

Specimen plaice
from the channel at Greenfield

CALDY, Wirral

A match fishing venue with a good reputation for flounder

Caldy is a popular match venue on the eastern shore of the Dee estuary between Heswall and West Kirby. From the low water mark to half tide the beach is mostly mud giving way to sand and a few patches of stone towards high water. It is sheltered from all but northwesterly winds.

How to Get There

Leave the M56 at J15 then take the A540 following the signs to Hoylake. A few miles past Heswall turn left at the roundabout onto the B5140 (Caldy Road). As you pass through Caldy Village the left hand fork, just past the church, takes you onto Croft Drive East with the turn off to the beach and Croft Drive 50 yards further along on the right. Parking is available at the Wirral Country Park 100m from the access to the beach but it locked at night so check the noticeboard.

What & When

Sport is slow during January and February apart from rockling and the occasional large flounder leaving the estuary prior to spawning. Towards the end of March the

Shore Marks

flounder return and although many of the fish are out of condition some still top the 1lb 12oz (0.8 kg) mark. Catches of flounder peak in May and early June when good bags around 12oz to 1lb 8oz (0.3 to 0.7 kg) are common. More recently plaice are being caught in increasing numbers and on some tides can be as prolific as the flounder. They average around the 1lb (0.45kg) mark with better fish to 2lb (0.9kg) a possibility. Eels also show at this time of year and along with flounder and a few school bass make up the bulk of summer catches. By the start of October catches are limited to whiting on night tides and flounder which are fewer in number than earlier in the year but of a much better size and up until the turn of the year present the angler with a chance of a specimen in excess of 2lb (0.9 kg).

How to Catch Them

Tides in the 8.5 to 9.5m (Liverpool) range tend to out fish neap tides. Arrange to start the session about three hours before high tide just as the water starts to flood quickly over this shallow beach. Casting out and walking back with the tide is a very effective method until the tide pushes you onto the the coastal defence which also marks the limit of high water. Over high water the fish are usually feeding between 60 and 90 yards (55 and 85m) of the beach but can sometimes be located at short range working the stones just below the high water mark. As the tide starts to ebb the fish move further out favouring the long casters but even they can't reach them after around 2 hours of the ebb. This mark fishes best during moderate southwesterlies.

TACKLE

There is a fair amount of run on the early ebb on springs but a 5 to 6oz (140 to 170g) grip will serve to hold bottom on most occasions. Size 1 Aberdeens fished on a 3-hook nylon paternoster rig (see Rig Guide) score well here with 5 to 6oz (140 to 170g) breakaway leads easily coping with a moderate tide run and any drift due to a side on wind.

BAIT

Ragworm is productive at the start and end of the year but as the weather warms up and crabs become more active then peeler becomes essential. Early in the season tipping the crab or worm bait off with a long piece of mackerel can out fish a plain bait.

[Opposite] Bob Murphy with a match-winning bag of the prized Dee flounder from Caldy beach.

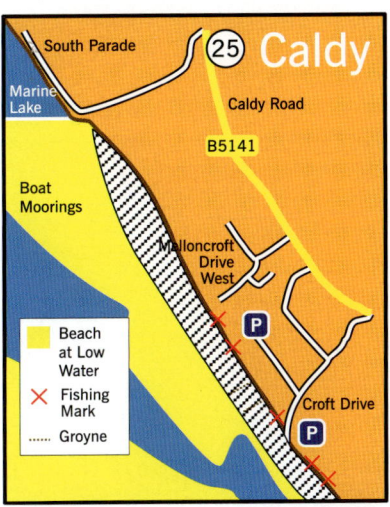

O.S. Map Sheet No. 108
Admiralty Chart No. 1978
High water: Liverpool -0hr 50
Usually: Access: 2 Comfort: 2
Spring HW: Access: 2 Comfort: 3
(See ratings at foot of page 7)

TOP TIP

When using crab or worm bait, tipping it off with a long strip of mackerel will improve the catch rate during the early part of the season.

KING'S PARADE, Wirral

Easy access, comfortable fishing, free parking and fish!

Kings Parade is part of the promenade which runs along the north coast of the Wirral. The selected marks are at the New Brighton end where the main road runs adjacent to the promenade.

How to get There
Follow the M53 all the way to J1 then follow the A554 which leads on to the promenade.

What & When
Sport is very poor at the start of the year but begins to improve early in April as plaice move into the Rock Channel which runs parallel to the shore line. The double slipway at the New Brighton end of the promenade is favourite especially when fished on the first 2 hours of the flood up the beach and for another hour on the promenade. Neap to medium sized tides are essential as the low water channel all but dries up on springs. The plaice average around the 1lb (0.45kg) mark but larger fish to 3lb (1.35kg) are reported on occasion. Flounder are another species that can be expected with small codling and the odd dogfish when high water coincides with

Plenty of good whiting in October.

••• Shore Marks •••

The promenade has all the accessibility of a public road with free parking and comfortable fishing. It is very suitable for anglers with restricted mobility

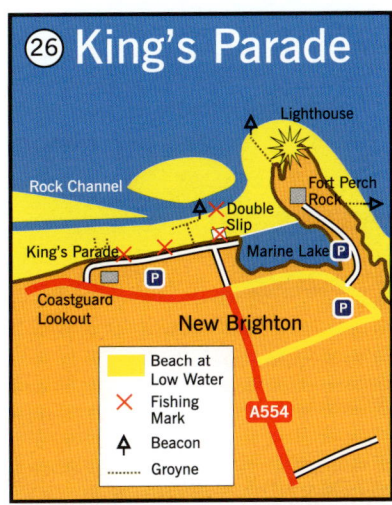

darkness. Bass start to appear during May. Fish will be taken from the promenade over high water but better catches can be expected fishing the first 2 hours of the flood. Most fish are in the 2 to 4lb (0.9 to 1.8kg) range but larger fish to 7lb (3.2kg) have been taken. The past few years have seen an increasing number of thornback especially over the low water period. Small fish to 6 lb (2.7kg) predominate but specimens to 12lb (5.5kg) have been reported. Smoothound have also started to show with several fish over 10lb (4.5kg) landed. Large baits work best for both species with soft crab and squid on a pennel rig the favoured method. These species plus a few silver eels make up the bulk of sport throughout the summer although a prolonged settled spell in July and August can bring mackerel and launce within casting range. Whiting arrive as September draws to a close and their numbers peak in October and early November. Dabs and the occasional in size codling stay with the whiting until the end of the year when results taper out to nothing. ***Take care when fishing the flood tide to avoid being cut off by the gulleys filling in behind.***

How to Catch Them

The concrete groynes that run at right angles to the promenade allow most tides to be fished with 4 or 5oz (110 or 140g) grip leads. Do not fish from the groynes as they are submerged on all but the smallest tides

BAIT

Ragworm and lugworm are productive early in the year but from May through to October peeler is the preferred bait. Once the water cools off and crab activity slows down then worm and fish baits will once again start to produce

TACKLE

A traditional nylon paternoster 2- or 3-hook rig (see Rig Section) armed with size 2 or 1 Aberdeen style hooks work well when fishing the tide in from low water and over high. A clipped down 1 hook rig fished at distance from the promenade will often pick out fish while those fishing closer are struggling.

O.S. Map Sheet No. 108
Admiralty Chart No. 1978
High water: Liverpool –0hr 17
Access: 1 Comfort: 1
(See ratings at foot of page 7)

STAR CATCH

Wallasey angler Mark Cornah landed a smoothound of 14lb 6oz (6.5kg) in June 2005 which is believed to be a local record.

PERCH ROCK, New Brighton

A very popular low water mark

On the tip of the Wirral Peninsula, Perch Rock Bank is the sandbank associated with a large rock outcrop at the mouth of the Mersey estuary. It is the site of a well-known fort and can be fished in most weathers although a strong wind from the west can have the sand whistling about.

How to Get There

Leave the M53 at J1 taking the A554 following signs for New Brighton. After 2 miles turn right on to the promenade and follow for 1 mile before parking adjacent to Perch Rock Fort. There is ample free parking within a few hundred yards of the beach.

What & When

Early in the year the bank produces good numbers of dabs in the 8 to 12oz (0.2 to 0.3kg) range with a few topping the 1lb (0.45kg) mark. Whiting can also be expected right through into March when catches drop off. Sport remains slow until late April when the first crab moult triggers an improvement in results. Flounder are the first to show, closely followed by plaice, eels, dabs and the occasional dogfish. These species provide the bulk of catches throughout the summer although whiting, school bass and small gurnard may also feature. Mullet are also in evidence but as very few anglers fish for them their potential has yet to be fully realised. September sees the return of the whiting shoals which dominate returns throughout the remainder of the winter. Codling are few and far between but if they do put in an appearance it will be most likely at the southern end of the bank opposite Victoria Road. Recent years have seen thornback move into the river and although not as prolific as in other areas of the Mersey there have been a number of fish over 10lb (4.5kg) landed. April until the end of September seems to be most productive although they have been taken outside this period.

How to Catch Them

The venue can only be fished over the low water period as the flooding tide pushes you beyond casting range of the main channel. Aim to start your session a couple of hours

Shore Marks

before low water and finish an hour up the flood. The increasing tidal flow and rubbish gathering on the line makes fishing beyond this period difficult.

TACKLE

Although the bottom is fairly clear, the seabed undulations can foul the end tackle so a medium power rod with at least 15lb (7kg) BS line is needed to bully your way in. A 1-up 1-down rig fixed to the bottom with a 5 or 6oz (140 or 170g) breakaway to counter a fairly strong tide run is a popular choice. Hook sizes range from 2 to 2/0 depending on the species targeted.

BAIT

Lug, rag and mackerel are all excellent choices during the colder months but crab is essential in summer.

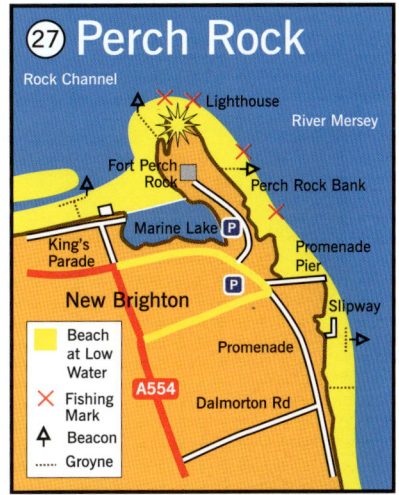

27 **Perch Rock**

O.S. Map Sheet No. 108
Admiralty Chart No. 1978
High water: Liverpool –0hr 00
Access: 2 Comfort: 2
(See ratings at foot of page 7)

STAR CATCH

Wirral angler Terry Wallworth caught three thornback scaling between 8lb (3.6kg) and 12lb 6oz (5.6kg) in one session during September 2005

A quality Mersey plaice.

65

EGREMONT, Wallasey

A good chance of decent cod from the vent shaft area

This mark, on the Wirral side of the ersey covers the promenade from Vale Park to Seacombe Ferry. Sand at the base of the promenade gives way to a mixed bottom of stone, mussel beds and mud.

How to Get There

Leave the M53 at J1 following the signs for Wallasey Docks. Take the A5139 (Dock Road) to the roundabout then turn left onto the A554. Turn right at the next roundabout and park on the left hand side of the ferry if fishing the southern end of the promenade. If fishing the northern section go left on to Brighton Street and park either alongside the Guinea Gap pool in River View Road or at the bottom of Tobin Street.

What & When

Results are poor during the first few months of the year and catches don't improve until April when a few codling, mostly undersized, dabs and flounder start to show. Sport is in full swing by the start of May with the flats increasing in numbers and being joined by eels and plaice. The plaice average around 1lb (0.45kg) with a few fish over 2lb (0.9kg) taken on occasion. Results hold up during June and early July but tail off with the approach of August. They pick up again towards the end of September with the arrival of whiting. October sees the best of the fishing when catches are dominated by whiting in the 8 to 12oz (0.2 to 0.3kg) range, dabs and the odd flounder and plaice. By the end of October flounder and plaice are few and far between but codling move into the river to fill the void. Mostly fish in the 1lb 4oz to 2lb (0.6 to 0.9kg) range but some years see much larger fish into double figures landed especially from the vent shaft area. Numbers of whiting and dab drop off towards the end of December but the codling can be at their best later in the year.

How to Catch Them

The building of three new breakwaters between Tobin Street and Dalmorton Road has had a profound effect on the tide by reducing the flow on the flood especially the section between Tobin Street and the Guinea Gap baths. The effect on the ebb is less noticeable and in common with many marks in the Mersey there are times on spring tides

Shore Marks

when it becomes almost impossible to hold bottom especially towards Seacombe ferry where the tide is strongest. The preferred tides are those between 8.0 and 9.0m at Liverpool.

TACKLE

A medium to heavy beachcaster matched with an equivalent reel loaded with 18lb (8kg) BS line is perfect to combat the tide and any fish encountered. 40 to 50lb (18 to 22.5kg) shock leaders act as good insurance against any abrasions suffered over the small stones and mussel beds that make up the sea bed along this stretch. 5 to 6oz (140 to 170g) breakaway leads and a range of hooks from size 1 to 2/0 complete the outfit.

BAIT

During the period April to October the main bait is peeler crab with lug and rag accounting for fish when crab activity is at a minimum. Mackerel strip is very effective for whiting once they show in September. Lugworm is excellent for late season dabs and a good second choice to peeler crab for codling.

Eels feature regularly in the summer catches at Egremont.

O.S. Map Sheet No. 108
Admiralty Chart No. 1978
High water: Liverpool −0hr 00
Access: 1 Comfort: 1
(See ratings at foot of page 7)

✱ TOP TIP

Tackle losses can be expected, especially towards the vent shaft, but they can be reduced by using a shock leader to reduce the effect of abrasion on the sea bed.

67

WOODSIDE, Birkenhead

A summer hotspot for mullet

ituated on the Wirral side of the River Mersey the promenade at Woodside runs from the ferry south for about 400 yards (370m towards Cammell Lairds (now Northwestern Shiprepairers). The sea bed is mainly sand, mud and stone, however the section directly behind the car park can be very snaggy due to the landing stage mooring chains. There is also 100 yards of promenade that can be fished to the north of the of the ferry stretching between the tunnel vent and the landing stage. This stretch can also be very snaggy but is less so towards the vent. The promenade is well sheltered from winds from the west but can become uncomfortable but still fishable with winds from the south east and north west.

How to Get There

Take J1 off the M53 and follow the signs for Wallasey Docks before joining the Dock Road (A5139). At the next roundabout turn right following signs for Woodside Mersey Ferries. There is a pay and display car park to the right of the landing stage allowing parking within yards of the sea wall.

What & When

January may see a few codling, dabs and whiting taken but by the end of the month through to the end of March sport will be in a decline which doesn't improve until April. Then a run of small codling appears in the river with a few larger fish around the 1lb 8oz (0.7kg) mark amongst them. Dabs will also feature well in catches and as the month progresses and the main peel of crab gets underway they are joined by flounder, plaice and eels. These 4 species dominate summer catches and as a result this section of new promenade has become popular with match fisherman. More recently mullet have also featured in catches especially towards the sewer outlet and several fish over 4lb (1.8kg) have been landed. Sport goes into a decline through September but picks up dramatically late in the month with the arrival of whiting in the 8 to 12oz (0.2 to 0.3kg) range with a few larger fish over 1lb (0.45kg) in with them. Codling put in another appearance at the end of October and along with the whiting and dabs make for excellent sport during November and December.

Shore Marks

The promenade is clean, modern and safe. It easily meets the access requirements of disabled anglers. The car park serving the ferry landing is very convenient for the promenade itself.

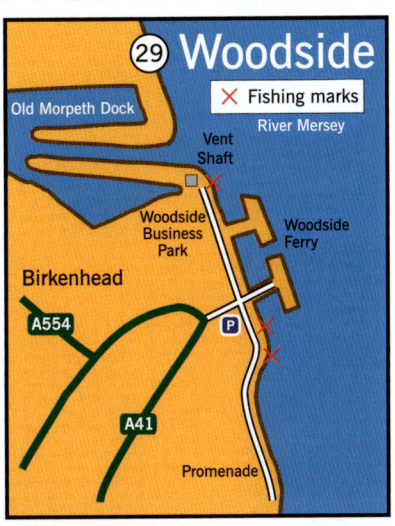

The author with a good mullet caught at Birkenhead

How to Catch Them

Although fish will be taken over high water the mark is more productive in the last 3 hours of the ebb and first 2 of the flood. The tides in the Mersey are very strong and although you can fish for a short period on the larger tides its best to choose a tide in the 8 to 9 metre range when its possible to hold bottom with 5 to 6oz (140 to 170g) grip leads.

TACKLE

The choice of tackle is governed to a certain extent by the strong tidal run that prevails. 18lb (8kg) BS main line to a 50 or 60lb (22 or 27kg) BS shock leader is required for distance work while at short range 25lb (11kg) BS right through has the advantage that the build up of rubbish around the leader knot is eliminated. The disadvantage of the heavier line is increased drag due to tide although this can be reduced by using a braided line. Throughout the summer months a 1-up 1-down rig tied to size 4 to size 1 hooks is favoured but during the winter season with codling and whiting the quarry it pays to scale up hook size to accommodate the larger baits.

BAIT

Peeler crab is a must during the summer months but later in the year fish baits and black lug can be very productive. However, crab fresh or good frozen tends to account for the better bags of codling.

O.S. Map Sheet No. 108
Admiralty Chart No. 1978
High water: Liverpool −0hr 00
Access: 2 Comfort: 1
(See ratings at foot of page 7)

STAR CATCH

The N.W.A.S.A.C. thick lipped grey mullet record of 4lb 12oz (2.15kg) was caught here by John Waugh in 1995 using bread flake as bait.

BROMBOROUGH

A favourite match venue on the Mersey

 On the Wirral coast between Tranmere and Eastham, the Old Dock Wall at Bromborough has become a popular match venue.

How to Get There

Head north along the A41 from junction 5 off the M53 and turn right into Port Causeway at the traffic lights 1 mile past Bromborough Retail Park. Turn left into Dock Road South and park half a mile down, just before the road bears sharp left. A track runs from the gate for 150m to the dock wall.

What and When

Although fishable at all stages of the tide, the wall dries out on all but the smallest tides leaving a swathe of mud and sandstone ledges which extend well beyond the low water mark. Another feature is a rocky groyne, extending for 80m from the wall. The venue is backed by undergrowth, dense in places, which comes to within a metre of the wall. It is not unknown, especially in matches where space is at a premium, for anglers to pack a pair of secateurs to clear an area to fish.

Early January sees the tailing off of the cod season but the occasional larger fish can sometimes put in an appearance. By the end of the month the larger fish have moved out leaving undersized codling, rockling and a few whiting and dab. During February and March sport is very slow but results improve in April when silver eels and flounder move in. May and June see a continuing improvement with the flounder and eels increasing in numbers and size, some of the eels topping the 2lb (0.9kg) mark, while other species such as sole, sizeable codling and plaice occasionally appear in catches. These species stay throughout the summer and although mullet are often see feeding they are seldom fished for. September sees whiting appearing in catches and by the start of October they are well established. Flounder and eels will have all but disappeared by the middle of the month replaced in part by the first of the winter's codling. These tend to average around the 1lb 4oz to 2lb 4oz (0.5 -1.0kg)mark with the odd better sized fish in the 3lb to 6lb (1.4 - 2.8kg) range a possibility especially during December by which time the whiting shoals will have decreased in numbers. Dabs also show in catches during the winter but not in the same numbers as in other parts of the river.

⋯ Shore Marks ⋯

How to Catch Them

Tides at Bromborough are fierce and on the larger spring tides can be almost unfishable. Tides of 8 or 9m can be fished fairly comfortably with a 5 or 6oz (150 to 170g) breakaway lead but during the middle of the flood and ebb it may be necessary to cast "uptide" to hold bottom. Sandstone ridges can lead to tackle losses but a short move will often find cleaner ground. The wall is well sheltered from all but northerly winds. Although the low water period can be very productive, the mud between the wall and the low water mark can be off-putting so most anglers start a couple of hours after low, finishing an hour after high water. The start and end of the flood and slack water over high fish best for flounder, eels and whiting with cod favouring the middle 4 hours of the flood.

BAIT

Early season flounders and eels will often take lugworm or ragworm baits but by late spring the most productive bait is peeler crab. This remains so until the arrival of the whiting during September when fish baits or worm and fish cocktails become increasingly effective. Lugworm works well for winter codling but peeler crab is usually more productive.

TACKLE

A 2- or 3-hook paternoster rig loaded with size 2 to 1/0 hooks fished between 10 and 80m is the preferred method for all bar the codling which prefer a bait offered in the 100 to 140 m range where the water is deeper and, more importantly, faster flowing. An "up and down" pennel rig with size 3/0 hooks clipped down is ideal for this allowing a large bait to be fished at distance.

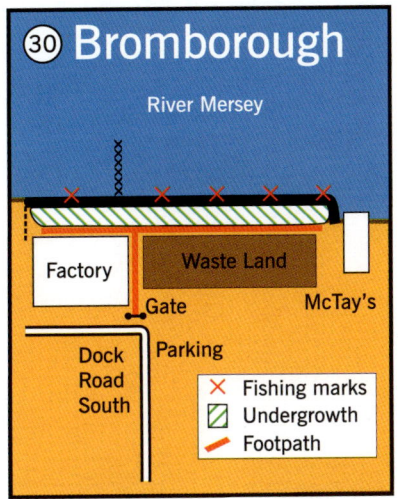

O.S. Map Sheet No. 108
Admiralty Chart No. 1978
High water: Liverpool −0hr 00
Access: 2 Comfort: 1
(See ratings at foot of page 7)

Phil Simpson with a 7lb 2oz (3.25kg) cod from Bromborough

❗ SAFETY ANGLE

Brambles and hidden mooring rings skirt the edge of the wall and present a tripping hazard so take care approaching the water's edge, particularly in the wet.

71

OTTERSPOOL

Sea angling in the suburbs

 unning almost two miles from Garston to South Liverpool docks Otterspool promenade was opened in 1950 and extended during the latter part of the millennium. As well as being a comfortable venue with easy access it also hosts many matches including the prestigious S.A.M.F Masters. The more favoured section is the part fronting the former Garden Festival site though fishing is good the entire length of the promenade.

How to Get There

From the M56 at junction 12 take the A557 towards Widnes and cross the Runcorn Bridge onto the A562. Follow this road through Speke and on to the A561, St Mary's Road then Aigburth Road. At Aigburth Vale follow the sign and go left down Jericho Lane to the promenade and car parks. Smooth, gently sloping paths lead from the plentiful car parks to the water's edge.

From the dock exit of the Queensway Tunnel turn onto the A5036 passing the Liver Building and Albert Dock before bearing right at the traffic lights at the junction of Parliament Street and onto Sefton Street. A further couple of miles further on Sefton Street joins the promenade at Riverside Drive. There is ample parking on both sides of the road just before the Britannia Pub.

What and When

From April through to September the venue produces good bags of flounder and silver eel with dabs, small codling and the occasional sole also putting in an appearance. As the weather starts to cool during late September then whiting move within casting range. Numbers increase as winter approaches with double figure bags of fish in the 12oz to 1lb (0.3 - 0.45kg) range common. Larger fish to 2lb (1kg) are caught on occasion. Codling start to show in October and fish can be expected right through into the New Year. Fish in the 1lb 8oz to 3lb (0.7 - 1.4kg) range are the norm but like a number of Mersey venues larger fish into double figures are taken on occasion. Decent bags of whiting and codling can still be anticipated well into February but catches drop off during March.

Shore Marks

How to Catch Them

Strong tidal flow, especially on the ebb, in this section of the River dictates that the most comfortable and successful period to fish is on the flood. Aim to start your session a couple of hours after low water and finish just after high when the ebb starts to pick up.

TACKLE

A 1 up, 1 down rig loaded with size 2 to 1 hooks offered at between 20 and 60m is a tried and trusted method although a larger bait and hook can be more successful especially for winter codling. A 5 or 6oz (150 - 170g) breakaway lead will be needed to combat the tide and even heavier again if casting further. The bottom is stone and mussel and is relatively snag free although rubble at the base of the wall can cause problems.

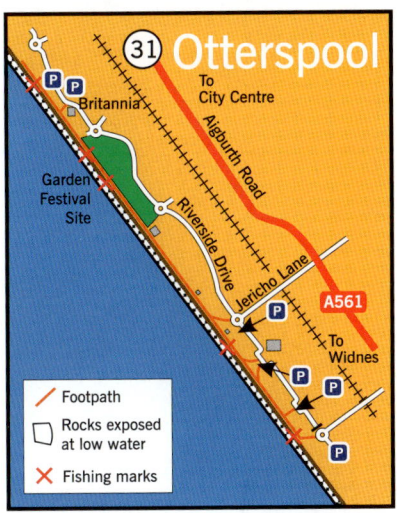

Visiting Manx angler Mike Emery with a February codling at Otterspool

O.S. Map Sheet No. 108
Admiralty Chart No. 1978
High water: Liverpool –0hr 00
Access: 1 Comfort: 1
(See ratings at foot of page 7)

BAIT

Peeler is by far the best bait during the summer months and although still successful during the winter, especially for codling, its importance is not as great, as lesser baits such as mackerel; lug and ragworm become more effective.

ALEXANDRA DOCK, Liverpool

First class fishing at the heart of Liverpool Docks

lexandra Dock Wall is between Seaforth rocks and Langton dock. The venue is 550 yards (600m) long in two parts. The Langton end has a parapet with a 4ft (1.3m) wall in front while the Gladstone end has a parapet with a similar wall behind. The Langton end is safer, especially for children, but it is harder to land large fish. The Gladstone end is easier to fish but has a 6ft (1.8m) wide ledge to a 40ft (12.3m) sheer drop at low water. The mark is quite sheltered but the water breaks over the wall in winds over force 5 from the west to north. The sea bed is sand, mud and small stones with patches of mussel. *A permit is required for this mark.*

How to Get There

From the Wallasey (Kingsway) Tunnel exit follow the A59 north for half a mile before forking left into Stanley Road. At the junction with Boundary Street turn left before turning right into Derby Road (A565). Follow the A565 for a mile and a half then take a left turn into Strand Road. The dock entrance is at the bottom of this road. This entrance is open from 06.30 until 19.15. Outside these hours access is via the Crosby Road South entrance at Seaforth.

What & When

The year starts with codling at 1 to 3 lb (0.45 to 1.35kg), whiting and dabs but as spring approaches catches start to tail off. In March and April small codling join the whiting that remain. Dogfish show from time to time. Flounder and eels also arrive in April and catches peak in June and July. The flounders are a good size, 12oz to 1lb 4oz (0.3 to 0.6kg) and some of the bigger eels reach 2lb (0.9kg). Dabs will also be taken in good numbers with whiting, sole and occasional school bass also appearing. The main whiting shoals arrive in September dominating catches through to December. They are a good size, many around 12oz to 1lb (0.3 to 0.45kg) and a few around 2lb (0.9kg) taken most years. The show of codling will vary depending on that year's run of fish and although most are around 1lb 8oz to 2lb 8oz (0.7 to 1.1kg, larger fish are always possible so a drop net is advisable.

How to Catch Them

Most species here feed best over slack water with codling, which favour the start or finish of the tide being the exception.

Shore Marks

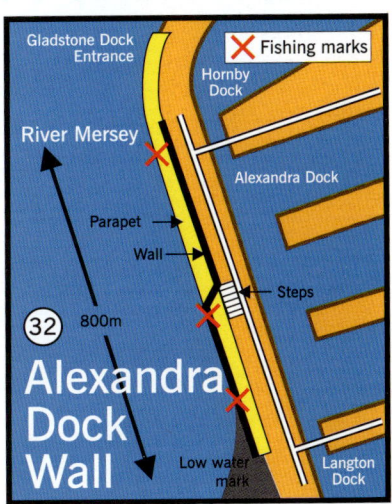

OBTAINING A PERMIT

Permits are issued on personal application. Telephone 0151-949 6144 for an appointment. You will need photographic identity, such as UK driving licence or passport, a utility bill showing your name and address and proof of third party insurance, such as a membership of a fishing association that covers you whilst angling. Also have your vehicle's V5 (log book) or insurance certificate as a separate badge is required for your vehicle. The fee is £5 and covers until August 2007, you will then be required to renew the permit every two years.

TACKLE

A 1-up, 1-down rig with size 2 to 1 hooks fished between 10 and 80 yards (9 and 75m will usually score but larger baits on larger hooks will often produce better fish. A pennel rig with 3/0 hooks and a decent sized bait will take the bigger codling. Shock leaders, necessary for casting and reducing tackle losses, tend to accumulate material around the knot and so there has been a move to the strong, low diameter braids which at short range do not need a leader. For a couple of hours either side of low water a 5oz (150g) lead will hold bottom comfortably but as the tide increases grip leads are needed. On a neap tide a 170g) grip lead will hold through the flood and the ebb but spring tides will require heavier leads, the "sticky" Gemini leads coming into their own on occasion.

Dover sole from Alexandra Dock

O.S. Map Sheet No. 108
Admiralty Chart No. 1978
High water: Liverpool −0hr 00
By car: Access: 2 Comfort: 1
(See ratings at foot of page 7)

BAIT

From April to October the top bait is peeler crab for all species with worm and mackerel also quite effective at the start and end of this period. From the start of October through to February whiting and dabs will take fish baits and worm but any codling about usually favour crab, fresh or frozen.

ABOUT BOAT ANGLING

Go out there and catch the bigger fish

Boat Angling
CHARTER BOATS

Shore fishing is great sport but it's not the whole story, there are plenty more fish in the sea and the way to reach them is by boat.
Most anglers' first boat experience is usually as part of a group on a day charter vessel. This allows the beginner to fish with experienced anglers and learn the basics of boat angling. Charter vessels are often quite large and fast. They can reach distant marks quickly and handle offshore weather conditions. It can be expensive, especially in the more modern boats but chartering is often the only way to reach the big bags and specimen fish found on deep water wrecks and distant sandbanks.

YOUR OWN DINGHY

Many anglers, myself included, move from the daily charter to owning their own dinghy. Brought about to some extent by the desire to be independent, this allows the angler flexibility inthe timing, choice of venue and type of fishing to be undertaken without having to accommodate the views of the eight or nine other anglers on the boat.

SAFETY & BOATCRAFT

However, with this independence come responsibilities. Maintaining a boat can be time consuming and costly and towing, launching and recovery are skills that must be learnt. But most importantly the main responsibility is for the safety of yourself, crew members and other people afloat.
Fortunately there are several organisations that can help the small boat angler with advice and training.

The Royal Yachting Association runs navigation, boatcraft and radio operators courses while the RNLI has recently introduced their S.E.A. Check scheme whereby a local representative will (free of charge) check your vessel's safety equipment and offer advice on safety issues. The Coastguard also runs a Small Boat Register where details of the vessel, safety equipment and contact numbers are lodged with a local coastguard station for use in case of an emergency. (See Directory for more details of contacts for these schemes)
Remember the safer you feel, the more at ease you will be and the better you will enjoy your day afloat.

TREFOR SLIPWAY

Has the potential to threaten the UK record for bull huss

ying on the north coast of the Lleyn Peninsula, the slipway at Trefor gives access to the fishing marks in Caernarfon Bay. The sea bed at the inshore grounds, southwest to Porth Dinllaen and northeast as far as Dinas Dinlle, is mainly small reefs interspersed with patches of sand. Further out this gradually gives way to sand and stones then sand and shell. Tides over the inshore marks (within 2 miles of the shore) are gentle and rarely exceed 1 knot.

How to Get There

From Caernarfon take the A487 south, turning right at the A499 at Dinas. Follow the A499 for 14 miles before taking the turn signposted for Trefor. Follow this road for about half a mile or so then go sharp right towards the beach. This narrow road winds past a few cottages before emerging on the shoreline at the far side of the harbour and next to a large free car park. You will also find a limited amount of parking space is available adjacent to the slipway itself.

Local Conditions

LAUNCH & RECOVERY

The slipway is short and steep giving access to a beach launch off firm sand although it is possible to launch directly from the slip over high water on some of the larger tides. The beach is shallow so it is advisable when recovering to rope out your trailer. See Launch Charges panel on page 94 for details.

When launching, the harbour wall and land mass give protection from winds from any direction apart from those in the north to northeast quadrant. Also avoid recovery on low water springs as the low water mark extends beyond the harbour wall thereby losing its shelter from the west. Instead allow at least 1 hour up the flood before attempting to recover or launch.

HAZARDS

Avoid approaching the harbour from the north as a reef lies parallel to the harbour wall. Instead run in close to the small pier which extends out at right angles from the wall, avoiding the lines of anglers on the pier, before turning into the harbour.

Boat Marks

Enter Trefor harbour close to the pier to avoid the reef on the northern approach.

WEATHER

The Lleyn Peninsula shelters the inshore grounds from winds up to force 5 from the south through to east but the down draught from the Yr Eifl mountains can add 10 mph to winds from this quarter. Winds from the northeast and southwest are fishable up to force 4 but can be uncomfortable with the wind over the tide. Anything over force 3 from the north or west should be avoided.

TIDES

This part of Caernarfon Bay has a gentle tidal stream without any special problems.

What & When

Early season sport is limited to dabs, dogfish and whiting, improving during March as bull huss move inshore to spawn. Although overfishing in recent years seems to have reduced the average size, double figure fish can still be caught. Thornback ray also arrive in the spring, the grounds a couple of miles north of the harbour are the most prolific. At the end of April smoothhound start to show and by the end of May are well established, especially over the stony patches between Penrhyn Glas (Bird Rock) and Trwyn y Gorlech (The Crack). As a rule of thumb if you can just see Porth Ysgaden in line with the point at Porth Dinllaen then you are the right distance out. The smoothhounds take crab or worm baits and weigh around 4 to 6lb (1.8 to 2.75kg) with better sized fish into double figures (over 4.5kg) rare but possible. This mark also fishes well from the start of May for gurnard, dogfish, whiting and black bream. The bream are around 12oz (350g) and although specimens to just under 4lb (1.8kg) have been taken, anything over 1lb 8oz (0.7kg) is good. Mackerel show from the end of May building in numbers to the end of June when they are quite prolific. Tope predate heavily on these shoals and so the best of the tope fishing coincides with best of the mackerel

Boat Marks

fishing. Most are pack tope 10 to 20lb (4.5 to 9.0kg) but several over 35lb (16kg) are taken every year. The better marks are 4 to 5 miles northwest of Trefor so it is essential that sorties are only undertaken during more settled weather. Other species found in summer include tub and grey gurnard, dogfish, dabs, plaice, whiting, spotted and small-eyed ray with pollack, wrasse and coalfish from the rougher ground around Porth Dinllaen.

How to Catch Them

TACKLE
Choose an uptider in the 4 to 6oz (110-160g) casting range, Ambassadeur 6000 or 7000 loaded with 20lb (9.0kg) BS mainline attached to a 4 to 5oz (110-140g) weight. Tope and huss have abrasive skins so 20 feet (6m) of 50lb (22.5kg) BS leader will reduce fish loss.

BAIT
Mackerel, the fresher the better, peeler crab and lug, are the best baits although fresh whiting takes some beating for bull huss and thornback ray.

[Opposite] A specimen black bream for Wirral angler Richie Stead
[Below] Pete Behan with a double figure smoothhound

① Trefor Slipway

1 Rays, plaice, gurnard, dabs
2 Black bream, codling, dogfish, bull huss
3 Bull huss, dogfish, gurnard, smoothhound
4 Black bream, pollack, dogfish, smoothhound
5 Dogfish, rays, dabs, whiting, gurnard, tope

This sketch map is only to show the locations of the fishing grounds and must not be used for navigation purposes.

O.S. Map Sheet No. 123
Admiralty Chart No. 1970
High water: Liverpool –1hr 40

ⓘ Information

Garages with spacious forecourts on the A55 are open 24 hours making them ideal for topping up boat tanks. Toilets are in the harbour car park and also near the public telephone.

79

MENAI BRIDGE SLIPWAY

T he Menai Strait is served by a number of slipways but the most sheltered and popular is the slip at Menai Bridge, in Water Street between the bowling green and Porth Daniel Boat Storage.

How to Get There
Cross onto Anglesey via the Suspension Bridge (A5) then take the A545 at the first roundabout. Follow this road for 800 yards into the town of Menai Bridge then turn right at the crossroads into Water Street.

Local Conditions

LAUNCH & RECOVERY
Dinghies can be launched and recovered from the slip at any stage of the tide apart from an hour either side of low water on the bigger tides when the water is below the end of the slip. There is a limited amount of parking at the top of the slip and along Water Street. Parking is also available at Porth Daniel Boat Storage (Tel 01248 717784) at £5 per day. Launching is by permit. See the section on slipway charges on page 94 for details.

[Opposite] A fine plaice at 3lb 6oz (1.5kg), boat caught from Menai Strait

HAZARDS
Although the slipway is well sheltered except from the east, it is important that you are under power before leaving the launch site as the lateral tide run within yards of the slip can be very fast. A reef runs out at right angles to the shore just to the south west of the slip and is marked by a navigation beacon. Passage between the beacon and the shore should be avoided.

WEATHER CONDITIONS
The steeply wooded banks and narrowness of the central section between Menai Bridge and Porth Dinorwig is sheltered from winds from all bar the south west and north east but such is the local topography of this section that there is usually some protection to be had from all but the strongest winds. Outside these boundaries the land mass affords less shelter and as a result winds in excess of force 4 from the north east and south west, depending on which end is being fished, should be avoided and even less when the wind is over the tide.

Boat Marks

TIDES

The tide run close to the bridges can exceed 4 knots and reach 8 knots in the Swellies making this area unfishable for long periods of the tide. Away from here and each end of the Strait the tide run can be fast but for the most part fishable and while many avoid the spring tides it is these that produce the better fish. Tides between 8.7 and 9.3m Liverpool offer consistent results while tides below 8.0m have long periods of slack water and fewer fish.

What and When

From January to April catches are poor, mainly small codling, dabs and a few whiting. Results start to improve in late April, with the first major peel of shore crab with flounder, dogfish, whiting and codling appearing in catches. The codling tend to be small, 10 to 12 in. (25 to 30cm) on average, although fish in the 1lb 4oz to 1lb 12oz (0.6 to 0.8kg) bracket can be anticipated right through the summer. Flounder fishing, especially around the Caernarfon and Fforyd areas, can be exceptional at this time of year with many fish over 1lb 8oz (0.7kg). 1998 saw specimens over 2lb (0.9kg) including fish of 3lb and 3lb 2oz (1.35 and 1.4kg). The same period also sees an influx of herring, with the deep holes at Penmon and off Gallows Point favourite areas. Black bream move into the southwest end of the Strait early in July, populating the Plas Newydd area until September. The average size is around 6 to 12oz (170 to 340g) although this varies by year as does the number of better quality fish taken. My best was 2lb 5oz (1.05kg) and was one of three over 2lb (0.9kg) that year. However, local man Gary Mitchell beat this by a long way with a fish of 3lb 15oz (1.78kg) in the 1980's. Other species expected during the summer include tub gurnard, mackerel, ballan wrasse to 3lb 8oz (1.6kg) and plaice. Trigger fish can also turn up in late summer when the water is at its warmest. September sees another run of codling into the Strait with fish around 1lb 4oz to 3lb 4oz (0.6 to 1.5kg). Their numbers are greater than earlier in the year and 20 to 30 fish in a session is not uncommon, especially during October when sport is at its best. Larger fish do show occasionally with authentic catch reports of several fish weighing between 7 and 10lb (3.2 and 4.5kg), topped by specimens of 14lb and 17lb (6.35 and 7.7kg) both taken from the deep water near Pwllfanogl. Whiting and dabs will also be at their best at this time of the year with both these species favouring the sandier areas off Porth Dinorwig and between Gallows Point and Lleiniog. This latter area enjoys a reputation for specimen dabs with fish of 1lb 9oz, 1lb 13oz and 2lb (0.7kg, 0.8kg and 0.9kg) recorded. The Strait can fish well right through until the middle of December given favourable weather conditions but an influx of snow water from the nearby Snowdon range, and consequently a drop in sea temperature, can bring a premature end to the season.

Boat Marks

How to Catch Them

TACKLE
The Strait with its fast tides and shallow depths lends itself to uptiding so all rigs associated with this method of fishing can be employed. During periods of the tide when it is comfortable to fish under the boat, it often pays to offer baits above the bottom as during these conditions fish are often to be found higher in the water. At this time a shrimp rig tipped with small pieces of bait can be excellent especially for black bream, codling, whiting, pout and dabs.

BAIT
Lugworm, ragworm, mussel and cockle are good when crabs are at their least active or when fish are plentiful, but on any other occasion peeler crab will prove more productive and resilient.

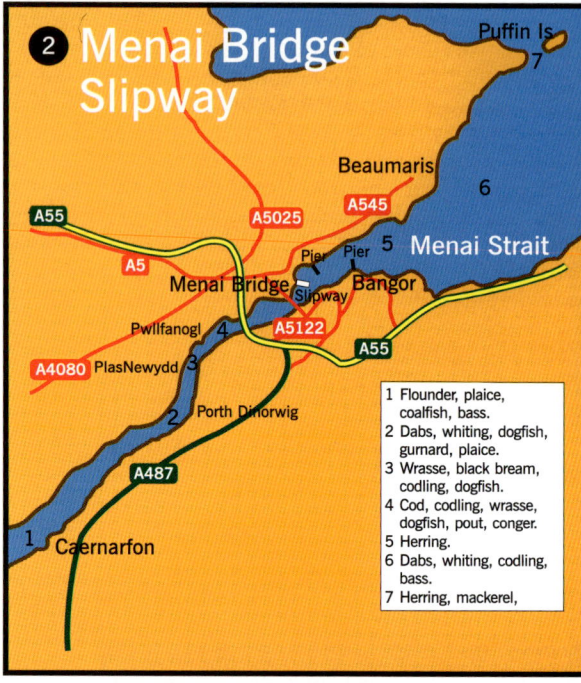

1 Flounder, plaice, coalfish, bass.
2 Dabs, whiting, dogfish, gurnard, plaice.
3 Wrasse, black bream, codling, dogfish.
4 Cod, codling, wrasse, dogfish, pout, conger.
5 Herring.
6 Dabs, whiting, codling, bass.
7 Herring, mackerel.

This sketch map is to show the locations of the fishing grounds only and must not be used for navigation purposes.

The author with a trigger fish from the Menai Strait

O.S. Map Sheet No. 114
Admiralty Chart No. 1464
High water: Liverpool −0hr 30

Information

The nearest garage is on the roundabout ½ mile past A545 turn-off. The nearest telephone is opposite the Bulkeley Arms in Menai Bridge. Public toilets are in Menai Bridge.

TREARDDUR BAY SLIPWAY, Anglesey

Trearddur Bay is the name of a town, a beach and a stretch of water on the south coast of Holy Island. Its pleasant aspect, safe, clean beaches and the convenience of nearby Holyhead combine make it a very a popular holiday spot. It also has a very good launch site.

How to Get There
From the A5 at Valley take the B4545 over Four Mile Bridge into Trearddur Bay before turning left after the Bay Hotel. The slipway is opposite the Trearddur Bay Hotel with parking for slipway users 150metres on.

Local Conditions
LAUNCH & RECOVERY
Launching is possible directly from the slip for a short period over high water but most of the time it is from the beach. The sand is firm so launching should not be a problem although after a series of neap tides the sand at the bottom of the slip can become soft and easily churned up making the slip difficult to use without four wheel drive. Launching requires a permit. See Launch Charges panel on page 94 for details.

HAZARDS
There are a number of small reefs scattered across the beach which cover on spring tides but they are easy to see and avoid. Take care also to avoid mooring ropes, especially during the holiday season.

WEATHER
The beach and the surrounding coastline face west so any wind more than a breeze from the south or west makes boating difficult or dangerous. Holy Island shelters the area from northerlies and easterlies but avoid fishing in winds over force 4.

TIDES
High water is roughly 1 hour and 15 minutes before Liverpool. The area within a line drawn between Porthdafarch and Rhoscolyn Head is fishable at all stages of the tide but once outside this line the run can be fierce especially around the headlands at South Stack and Penrhyn Mawr where fishing is limited to an hour or so either side of high and low water on the larger tides.

Boat Marks

A good 8lb (3.63 kg) thornback ray caught in Trearddur Bay

What & When

The sea bed in the area is a mixture of sand and reef and attracts an excellent variety of species throughout the year. Between January and March the inshore reefs draw codling in the 2 to 3lb (0.9 to 1.35 kg) range plus a few larger fish to 8lb (3.6 kg). Coalfish to 4lb (1.8 kg) are also taken as are small pollack and dogfish. Rays can be expected over the cleaner ground from the end of February, mostly thornback at first, but as the season progresses they are joined by spotted, blonde, small eyed and an occasional cuckoo ray. The most productive areas have been Rhoscolyn Head and a few miles further south off Rhosneigr, where the past few years have seen a number of specimen rays boated including a thornback of 19lb 4oz (8.75 kg), a blonde ray of 26lb (11.8kg) and a number of spotted ray over 4lb (1.8 kg). Bull huss, whiting, dabs and the odd plaice will also feature early in the year as will mackerel, usually appearing off Porthdafarch from the middle of April. Sport is in full swing by the middle of May with red, tub and grey gurnard along with smoothhound adding to the already established species. The smoothhound are not as prolific as those off Trefor but they seem to be of a better size, a fact highlighted by the Welsh record fish of 10.54 kg that was boated in May 2002. Settled weather during the summer months sees dinghies heading out to Careg Hen, a reef which rises from 39 metres to just 6 metres. As a result of the fast tides and attendant overfalls the reef is best fished over the slack water period on small tides when pollack to 8lb (3.6 kg), coalfish to 4lb (1.8 kg) and codling to 6lb (2.7 kg) can be expected on the drift with conger and large bull huss showing while at anchor. Into October the dominant species are whiting, dabs and dogfish over the sandier areas out from Rhosneigr with coalfish, pollack and codling over the rougher ground off South Stack and Rhoscolyn.

How to Catch Them

Drifting the reefs is a popular method of fishing the rougher ground with baited lures such as Hokkai and Shrimp rigs very productive. Over the cleaner ground the best of the rays are taken at anchor but drifting over the same ground will often produce better numbers of gurnard, plaice and dabs.

[Opposite] Pete Corker with a boat-caught spotted ray from Trearddur Bay

Boat Marks

TACKLE

An uptide rod capable of casting up to 6oz (170g coupled with an Ambassadeur 7000 loaded with 20lb BS monofilament line is an ideal combination for fishing over the inshore marks. However for the deeper water and more powerful tides further offshore a change to braided lines offers increased sensitivity and better bite detection.

BAIT

With the exception of smoothhound and wrasse which tend to prefer peeler crab, the top bait for the majority of the remaining species is fresh mackerel. The most likely area to find this bait is a couple of hundred yards off the aptly named Mackerel Rock at nearby Porthdafarch.

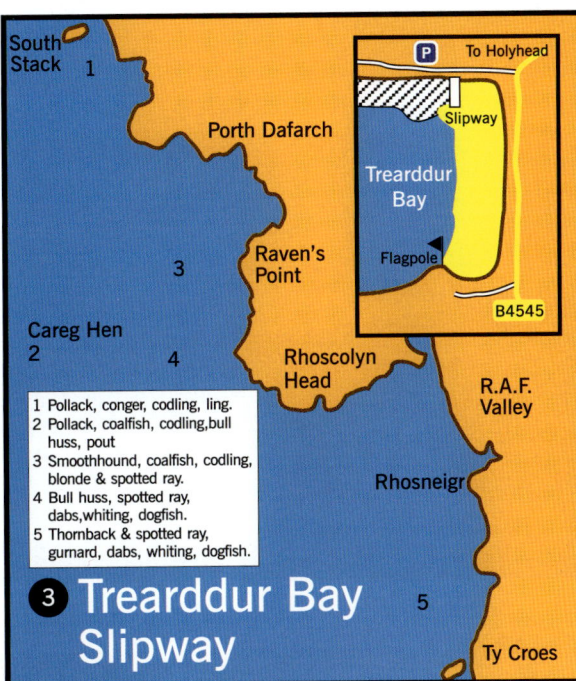

3 Trearddur Bay Slipway

1. Pollack, conger, codling, ling.
2. Pollack, coalfish, codling, bull huss, pout
3. Smoothhound, coalfish, codling, blonde & spotted ray.
4. Bull huss, spotted ray, dabs, whiting, dogfish.
5. Thornback & spotted ray, gurnard, dabs, whiting, dogfish.

This sketch map is to show the locations of the fishing grounds only and must not be used for navigation purposes.

O.S. Map Sheet No. 114
Admiralty Chart No. 1977
High water: Liverpool –1hr 15

ⓘ Information

There is a garage, telephone, general store, cafe and toilet at the turn-off to the slipway from the B4545 (Beach Road).

TRAETH BYCHAN SLIPWAY, Anglesey

Traeth Bychan is a pretty little beach situated on the east coast of Anglesey a couple of miles down the coast from the small port of Moelfre. It is popular with holiday makers and has all the amenities within a short distance of the launching slip.

How to Get There

After crossing onto Anglesey take the A5025 passing through Pentraeth and Benllech before turning right and down to the beach, at Marian-Glas. There is a large pay and display car park adjacent to the beach (£1.50 per day) although space can be at a premium during the holiday season and summer weekends.

Local Conditions

LAUNCH & RECOVERY

Launching, which is by permit (See Launch Charges panel on page 94 for details.) and recovery direct from the slipway is possible for 2 hours either side of high water and from the beach at other times. Care must be taken to avoid patches of soft sand. The beach is gently sloping around the low water mark so unless you have access to a tractor the best method of recovery is by roping out.

HAZARDS

Although the launch site is well sheltered from most directions, anything more than a breeze from the east should be avoided as it makes launch and recovery dangerous.

WEATHER

Facing east, the inshore marks are sheltered from the prevailing westerly winds by the Anglesey land mass and as a consequence the area has a reputation as a good back up venue if the more highly regarded west coast marks are unfishable.

TIDES

Tides over the inshore marks are fairly gentle but further offshore a run in the 1 to 2 knot range can be expected and there may be times when lead weights around the 1lb (0.45kg) mark are necessary.

Boat Marks

What & When

The area sees very little angling activity during the winter months but results from charter boats fishing at the inshore marks a few miles to the north and south would indicate that the whiting and dab fishing should be first class. From the start of April catches over the inshore marks are made up in the main of whiting in the 6 to 12oz (170 to 350g bracket, small codling, dabs and dogfish with herring and a few mackerel showing from the start of May. Smoothhound put in an appearance around the beginning of July and although not as abundant as those in Caernarfon Bay, they are in sufficient numbers to warrant a serious effort. They tend to average around the 6lb mark but larger fish up to 10lb (4.5 kg) are always a possibility. Peeler crab is by far the most successful bait, with

Quality tub gurnard can be expected from the offshore marks

Evening action off Traeth Bychan

Boat Marks

the deep water half a mile to the North East of Ynys Moelfre the most productive area. Mackerel are prolific from the start of July until the end of September and along with whiting, dogfish and a few dabs make up the bulk of catches from marks within a mile of the shore. Boats that work the reefs and rougher ground towards Point Lynas can expect pollack and wrasse with bass on occasion from the shallow waters surrounding Ynys Dulas. Dinghies that push out into the deeper water beyond the Four Fathom Bank during settled spells can be rewarded with good bottom fishing for thornback, tub gurnard, whiting, dabs, bull huss and the occasional tope during the summer months with quality dabs and whiting from the middle of September through to December.

This sketch map is to show the locations of the fishing grounds only and must not be used for navigation purposes.

How to Catch Them

TACKLE
Tackle for boat angling is fairly standardised in this area and the outfits described for the previous boat marks are also recommended for here.

BAIT
Fresh mackerel, readily available during the summer, takes some beating as an all round bait but varied levels of success can enjoyed with lug, cockle, squid and for the smoothhound, crab. Whole whiting can also be productive, especially for thornback.
There are extensive beds of lugworm on the beach and during the summer sandeel can be scraped from the sand at low water. There is a limited amount of peeler crab in the rocks on the left hand side of the beach.

O.S. Map Sheet No. 114
Admiralty Chart No. 1977
High water: Liverpool –0hr 25

ⓘ Information

There is a garage is in Benllech. The Beach Cafe is open in summer from 8am daily. It stocks some tackle. There is a public telephone in Marian Glas. The nearest toilets are in the car park behind the cafe.

NEW BRIGHTON SLIPWAY, Wirral

Although there are several slipways extending from the Wirral promenades into the River Mersey only the one at New Brighton is in use. a permit is required for launching. See Launch Charges panel on page 94 for details.

How to Get There

Leave the M53 at junction 1 and take the A554 following signs for New Brighton. After 1 mile the road emerges onto the promenade at which point turn right and follow the promenade until you pass the car parks at Fort Perch Rock. The slip is a couple of hundred yards further on at the bottom of Victoria Road. There is limited parking adjacent to the slip with plenty of free parking by the Fort.

Local Conditions

LAUNCH & RECOVERY

Although launching is possible direct from the slipway over high water on the larger tides it is mostly used as an access point for beach launching. This is possible at any time on tides below 8.0m at Liverpool but on larger tides this may have to be delayed, up to 2 hours before and after high water on big springs, until the water is clear of the slip. The sand is firm between the high and low water marks so launching with a car and roping out on recovery can be done without 4 wheel drive. However, the sand around the base of the slipway can be very soft so extra care must be taken when crossing onto the slip. You should avoid having to recover over this section unless you have 4 wheel drive.

HAZARDS

There is a concrete groyne running parallel to the low water mark just to the north of the launching area but due to it size is only a major problem in fog. However, to the south there is a sandstone reef which extends beyond the low water mark so aim to recover no more than 50 metres south of the groyne.

TIDES

With a 10 metre tidal range and a bottle neck at its entrance the Mersey can see tidal runs in excess of 5 knots on spring tides so most of the boat angling is carried out on tides of less than 8.6 metres when the run is still fierce but manageable.

Boat Marks

Local angler Andy Lunt with a 17lb (7.75kg) cod from the Mersey.

WEATHER

Fishing within the confines of the Mersey itself is comfortable in winds up to Force 5 from the south through to south west. Westerlies can also be fished but only for a few hours either side of low water when the sandbanks flanking the Rock Channel are exposed and offer shelter. The estuary is exposed from the west through to north so winds over Force 3 from this quadrant should be avoided. The Liverpool land mass provides shelter from easterly winds but while it may be comfortable to fish, be aware that the launching area can be choppy and if the wind increases significantly, dangerous on recovery.

What & When

January and February will see codling thinning out but enough will remain, bolstered by a few double figure fish, to make a cold day on the river worthwhile. Results tail off during March although the odd cod can still be expected until April. In fact April 2005 saw a 17lb 8oz (7.95kg) fish boated. Sport starts to improve as April progresses with plaice, flounder and dabs returning to the estuary. Some of the better marks at this stage of the season are amongst the moorings off Vale Park, the Woodside area, Seaforth and in the Rock Channel. Recent years have seen increasing numbers of thornback with Seaforth and the Rock Channel most productive. Smaller fish in the 2 to 5lb (0.9 - 2.3kg) range are the norm but double figure fish are not uncommon. The Rock Channel has also been good for smoothhound in the recent years and provides exciting sport in the shallow water during the last couple of hours of the ebb and first couple of the flood. These species along with silver eel, dogish, sole and tub gurnard will dominate catches throughout the summer until the whiting move inshore in September, their numbers peaking in November. They average around the 12oz (350g) mark with some of the better specimens nudging 1lb 8oz (0.7kg). C23 buoy, Perch Rock and Vale Park Bank are the better marks with the slack water period most productive. October sees codling starting to appear in catches and by the end of the month they are well established. Smaller fish in the 1lb 8oz to 3lb (0.7 - 1.5kg) range are the first to show followed by larger fish as we move into November. These early sorties usually produce good numbers of conger in the 5 to 10lb (2.3 - 4.5kg) range and thornback as they take baits intended for cod, especially over the rougher ground off Seaforth, the Clock Tower and Trafalgar Dock. As they start to thin out as the weather cools so the better sized cod start to show. Fish up to 8lb (3.6kg) are not uncommon with specimens well into double figures a possibility. Late November and December usually offer the best results.

Boat Marks

How to Catch Them

As a rule of thumb the best of the whiting and flatfish catches are over the slack water periods at high and low water with cod favouring the faster water at the start, end and middle of each flood and ebb.

TACKLE

The majority of fish are taken in 40 to 70ft – 12.5 to 21.5m of water and with the strong tidal flows the Mersey is ideal for uptiding. An Ambassadeur 7000 with 20lb (9kg) BS line with a 9.5ft (3m) rod capable of casting 6 to 8oz (170 to 200g) is an ideal choice of outfit. Rigs and hook size should be selected with the bait, species and size of fish in mind.

BAIT

From April to November the top bait is peeler crab. Fish baits and lugworm become more effective at the start and end of the year.

5 New Brighton Slipway

This sketch map is to show the locations of the fishing grounds only and must not be used for navigation purposes.

⚠ SAFETY ANGLE

Always fish within the buoys and never be tempted to pinch a few yards and anchor in the shipping channel because not only are the port authorities severe but the size and frequency of the shipping navigating the river make the practise very dangerous.

O.S. Map Sheet No. 114
Admiralty Chart No. 1978
High water: Liverpool –0hr 00

January 2006 saw a number of double-figure cod boated, topped by an new Mersey record fish of 27lb 13oz (12.4kg) caught by local man Dave Roberts.

What's the Record?

This is from the Rod Caught Record List of the Welsh Federation of Sea Anglers, whose area covers most of the marks in this book. The Wirral and Mersey marks are covered by the North West Federation of Sea Angling Clubs. The records are correct as of Spring 2007. Larger fish have been caught and were either unauthenticated or not reported. See the Directory for more details of how to report a catch for consideration in the record list.

Species	SHORE lb	oz	dr	Kg	Date	Location	BOAT lb	oz	dr	Kg	Date	Location
Bass	16	15	08	7.699	Jul 80	Aberthaw	15	00	02	6.808	Aug 97	Cardiff North
Bream, Black	4	00	01	1.816	2003	Criccieth	5	06	09	2.455	Jul 86	Langland Bay
Bream, Red					VACANT		1	04	04	0.575	Jun 81	Amlwch
Brill	1	07	07	0.665	Oct 90	Ravens Point	5	10	00	2.553	Jun 83	Milford Haven
Bull Huss	19	14	00	9.017	May 92	Pwllheli	20	08	00	9.300	Jun 84	Aberystwyth
Coalfish	7	02	00	3.232	May 94	Sker Rocks	17	08	00	7.938	Mar 82	Amlwch
Cod	44	08	00	20.186	Mar 76	Barry Island	45	08	00	20.640	Jan 97	Swansea Bay
Dab	2	09	08	1.178	Jul 36	Port Talbot	1	11	04	0.774	Nov 89	Beaumaris
Dogfish, Lesser Spotted	3	11	08	1.688	Nov 79	Fishguard	3	13	05	1.740	Nov 87	Mumbles
Eel, Conger	40	00	00	18.144	Jul 96	Port Talbot	60	14	00	27.615	Sep 96	Milford Haven
Flounder	3	14	08	1.772	Dec 86	Amroth	3	09	00	1.616	Sep 86	Beaumaris
Garfish	2	00	00	0.907	Oct 77	Anglesey	2	07	00	1.105	2001	Milford
Gurnard, Grey	1	00	14	0.478	May 87	Porthdafarch	1	13	09	0.838	2003	
Gurnard, Tub or Yellow	12	03	00	5.529	Aug 76	Langland Bay	9	01	10	4.129	Jun 84	Aberystwyth
Hake	3	08	02	1.592	Mar 84	Port Talbot	14	07	04	6.557	Jul 84	Milford Haven
Haddock	1	01	12	0.503	Jan 94	Watwick Steps	6	10	09	3.022	2004	Stout Point
Ling	9	00	08	4.097	Dec 84	Barry	31	07	00	14.260	Jan 80	Amlwch
Mackerel	4	04	14	1.953	Jul 90	Porthdafarch	2	08	02	1.139	Jul 79	Conwy
Mullet, Thick Lipped Grey	14	02	12	6.429	Oct 79	Aberthaw	6	03	13	2.830	Sep 94	Aberystwyth
Plaice	7	01	08	3.218	May 83	Deganwy	5	11	08	2.596	Jul 86	Oxwich Bay
Pollack	12	15	02	5.874	Dec 86	Port Talbot	22	00	00	9.979	Aug 91	Cardigan Bay
Pouting	2	11	00	1.221	Sep 80	Port Talbot	4	01	14	1.868	Nov 87	Swansea Bay
Ray, Blonde	30	01	00	13.637	Sep 93	Rhoscolyn	31	00	00	14.062	May 81	Amlwch
Ray, Cuckoo	4	07	13	2.037	Sep 81	Porthdafarch	5	10	00	2.553	Aug 97	Caernarfon
Ray, Small eyed	15	00	08	6.818	May 91	South Wales	15	02	00	6.861	May 84	Nash Sands
Ray, Spotted	8	05	00	3.771	Sep 80	Mewslade Bay	6	11	04	3.042	Apr 87	Nash Point
Ray, Thornback	18	01	04	8.200	2002	Barry	31	07	00	14.261	Jul 81	Liverpool Bay
Rockling, Three bearded	2	13	04	1.285	Aug 85	Anglesey	2	08	00	1.135	1969	Aberystwyth
Sea Scorpion, Short spined	1	00	12	0.475	Aug 98	Menai Strait	1	00	12	0.475	Dec 79	Menai Strait
Shark, Blue					VACANT		169	12	00	76.998	1999	Milford Haven
Shark, Porbeagle					VACANT		296	00	00	134.266	Jul 96	Porthcawl
Smoothhound, Common	15	12	12	7.167	Jul 81	Boverton	16	15	15	7.710	2004	Cardiff
Smoothhound, Starry	21	04	00	9.640	Sep 98	Aberthaw	23	03	12	10.540	2002	Trearddur Bay
Sole, Dover	4	03	00	1.900	Sep 91	Barry	3	06	01	1.534	Nov 89	Barry
Spurdog	13	03	06	5.993	May 79	Anglesey	17	15	00	8.139	Jul 80	Conwy
Tadpole Fish	1	02	14	0.535	Dec 76	Fishguard	0	15	02	0.431	Jun 76	Milford Haven
Tope	52	00	00	23.587	1999	Rhoscolyn	79	02	10	35.910	2005	Holyhead
Whiting	3	09	04	1.624	Nov 94	Cold Knap	3	10	14	1.671	Dec 97	Cardiff North
Wrasse, Ballan	6	08	09	2.966	Sep 77	Freshwater	4	13	00	2.185	Aug 78	Oxwich Bay
Wrasse, Cuckoo	1	08	00	0.682	Sep 86	St. Davids	1	15	04	0.888	Jul 97	West Dale Reef

MINI SPECIES

Species	Weight	Date	Location	Species	Weight	Date	Location
Blenny, Tompot	140g	2000	Fishguard	Poor Cod	305g	Dec 1982	Holyhead
Blenny, Yarrells	93g	Jul 1996	Ravens Point	Rockling, Shore	368g	Apr 1992	Dale
Goby, Painted	13g	Jul 1991	Holyhead	Weever, Lesser	80g	Jun 1989	Pendine
Goby, Rock	35g	Sep 1993	Caernarfon	Wrasse, Corkwing	290g		1999
Herring	372g	Jul 1983	Llam Carw	Wrasse, Goldsinny	102g	Jul 1995	Menai Strait
Pilchard	150g	Sep 1984	Milford Haven	Wrasse, Smallmouth	75g	Aug 1981	Holyhead

Conversion Tables

Select the number to convert in the middle column, read the conversion from the side.

Litres		Gallons
4.55	1	0.22
9.09	2	0.44
13.64	3	0.66
18.18	4	0.88
22.73	5	1.10
27.28	6	1.32
31.82	7	1.54
36.37	8	1.76
40.92	9	1.98
45.46	10	2.20

Metres		Feet
0.3	1	3.28
0.6	2	6.56
0.91	3	9.84
1.21	4	13.12
1.52	5	16.4
1.82	6	19.68
2.13	7	22.96
2.43	8	26.24
2.74	9	29.52
3.04	10	32.8
6.09	20	65.61
9.14	30	98.42
12.19	40	131.23
15.24	50	164.04
22.86	75	246.06
30.48	100	328.08

Nautical Miles		Statute Miles
0.86	1	1.15
1.73	2	2.30
2.60	3	3.45
3.47	4	4.60
4.34	5	5.75
5.21	6	6.90
6.08	7	8.05
6.95	8	9.20
7.82	9	10.35
8.68	10	11.50
13.03	15	17.26
17.37	20	23.01
21.72	25	28.76
43.44	50	57.53

Kilos	<Lb|Kg>	Lb	oz	dr
0.05	0.1	0	3	8
0.09	0.2	0	7	0
0.11	0.25	0	8	13
0.14	0.3	0	10	9
0.18	0.4	0	14	1
0.23	0.5	1	1	10
0.27	0.6	1	5	2
0.32	0.7	1	8	11
0.34	0.75	1	10	7
0.36	0.8	1	12	3
0.41	0.9	1	15	11
0.45	1	2	3	4
0.57	1.25	2	12	1
0.68	1.5	3	4	14
0.79	1.75	3	13	11
0.91	2	4	6	8
1.02	2.25	4	15	5
1.13	2.5	5	8	2
1.25	2.75	6	1	0
1.36	3	6	9	13
1.59	3.5	7	11	7
1.81	4	8	13	1
2.04	4.5	9	14	11
2.27	5	11	0	5
2.72	6	13	3	10
3.18	7	15	6	14
3.40	7.5	16	8	8
3.63	8	17	10	3
4.08	9	19	13	7
4.54	10	22	0	11
4.99	11	24	4	0
5.44	12	26	7	4
5.90	13	28	10	8
6.35	14	30	13	13
6.80	15	33	1	1
7.26	16	35	4	6
7.71	17	37	7	10
8.16	18	39	10	14
8.62	19	41	14	3
9.07	20	44	1	7
10.21	22.5	49	9	10
11.34	25	55	1	13
12.47	27.5	60	10	0
13.61	30	66	2	3
18.14	40	88	2	15
22.68	50	110	3	11

DIRECTORY

Emergency

For life in danger at sea or on the shore call
Coastguard..........999
VHF Channel 16

For dangerous objects found on the coast call the Local Authority, see page 96 for numbers

For any emergency call
Police 999
Ambulance...........999
Fire.......................999

Launch Charges

GWYNEDD for Trefor (also Pwllheli & Abersoch)
Documents required: Boat insurance certificate.
Registration fee: £20 if paid at launch site or £14 through Gwynedd County Council. Covers one year.
Daily charge: £12
Alternatively:-
Annual Permit: £124 inclusive of registration fee from council offices.
Application form: Council Offices, Caernarfon, LL55 1SH. Tel 01286 672255 www.gwynedd.gov.uk

ANGLESEY for Menai Bridge, Trearddur Bay & Traeth Bychan
Documents required: Boat insurance certificate.
Registration fee: £20 if paid at launch site or £13 through Anglesey County Council. Covers one year.
Daily charge: £12. *Monthly charge:* £80 *Yearly charge:* £120
Discounts: £40 for locals (Council Tax payers) £30 for holders of Level 2 Powerboat Certificate
Application form: Council Offices, Llangefni LL77 7TW. Tel 01248 752200 www.ynysmon.gov.uk

WIRRAL for New Brighton
Documents required: Boat insurance certificate. Car insurance certificate. Level 2 Powerboat Certificate. Two passport style photographs.
Annual permit: £110 or £50 if a member of a boat club. (ie powerboat, PWC or angling club).
Day ticket: £16.
Application form: Safewater Training, Victoria Parade, New Brighton CH45 2PH. Tel 0151-630 0466 Tractor launch available.

Tackle Shops

D & E Hughes,
Pwllheli 01758 613291

N. Wales Angling Centre
Caernarfon 01286 677099

Anglesey Bait Centre
Beaumaris 01248 852555

Latham's
Benllech 01248 712700

B.A.S.S.
Bangor 01248 355518

Ray's Tackle & Bait
Llandudno 01492 877678

Victoria Angling Centre
Colwyn Bay 01492 530663.

Geoff's Tackle & Bait
Rhyl 01745 356236

Foxon's Tackle
St Asaph 01745 583583

Fisherman's Cove
Ellesmere Pt 0151 356 9030

The Fisherman
Birkenhead 0151 653 4070

Moreton Angling Centre
Moreton 0151 677 8092

Ray's Tackle
Liverpool 0151 489 6103

Taskers Tackle
Liverpool 0151 260 6015

Johnson's Angling Centre
Liverpool 0151 525 5574

Hoppy's Angling Centre
Litherland 0151 928 5435

DIRECTORY

Tourism

North Wales Tourism
77 Conway Road
Colwyn Bay LL29 7LN
Tel 01492 531731
www.nwt.co.uk

Porthmadog T.I.C.
Y Ganolfan, High Street
Porthmadog
Gwynedd LL49 9LP
Tel 01766 512981

Caernarfon T.I.C.
Oriel Pendeitsh
Castle Street
Caernarfon LL55 1ES
Tel 01286 672232

Pwllheli T.I.C.
Min y Don, Station Square
Pwllheli, Gwynedd
LL53 5HG
Tel 01758 613000

Holyhead T.I.C.
Stena Line, Terminal 1
Holyhead
Anglesey LL65 1DQ
Tel 01407 762622

Bangor T.I.C.
Town Hall, Deiniol Road
Bangor, Gwynedd
LL57 2RE
Tel 01248 352786

Llandudno T.I.C.
1-2 Chapel Street
Llandudno
Conwy LL30 2YU
Tel 01492 876413

Colwyn Bay T.I.C.
Imperial Buildings
Princes Drive
Colwyn Bay LL29 8LF
Tel 01492 530478

Liverpool T.I.C.
Queen Square Centre
Liverpool L1 1RG
Tel 0906 680 6886 Prem rate
www.visitliverpool.com

National Organisations

Maritime & Coastguard Agency
Spring Place,
105 Commercial Road,
Southampton, SO15 1EG.
Tel 01703 329100.
24 hour information
service 0870 6006505
www.mcga.gov.uk
Government agency with responsibility for all aspects of sea safety and maritime emergencies.

Royal Life Saving Society UK
River House, High St,
Broom, Warks, B50 4HN
Tel 01789 773994
www.lifesavers.org.uk
Life saving and resuscitation training throughout the UK.

Royal Yachting Association
RYA House, Romsey Rd,
Eastleigh, SO15 9YA.
Tel 01703 627400
www.rya.org.uk
Governing body for boating in the UK. Provides advice and training courses for all types of recreational craft.

Royal National Lifeboat Institution
West Quay Road, Poole,
Dorset, BH15 1HZ
Tel 01202 663174.
www.rnli.org.uk
Voluntary organisation for the saving of life at sea. Provides free "Safety on the Sea" publications and other advice.

Environment Agency Wales

Environment Agency NW England
Tel 0800 80 70 60
www.environment-agency.gov.uk
Government agency with responsibility for the coastal environment.

Surfers Against Sewage
Rural Workshops,
Wheal Kitty, St Agnes,
Cornwall, TR5 0RD.
Tel 0845 458 3001
www.sas.org.uk
Campaign for clean, safe recreational water, free from sewage effluents, toxic chemicals, nuclear waste and marine litter.

Report Damage to the Coastal Environment

If you encounter pollution or any other environmental damage please call the **ENVIRONMENT AGENCY**
FREE 24 HOUR HOTLINE
0800 80 70 60

DIRECTORY

Angling

North West Association of Sea Angling Clubs
6 Corona Avenue, Lydiate,
Merseyside, L31 4DX
Tel 0151 526 0697
Co-ordinates sea angling clubs and events in the North West of England.
To claim a record catch in North West England contact Alan Marklew at the above address.

Welsh Federation of Sea Anglers
http://www.wfsa.org.uk
Co-ordinates sea angling clubs and events in Wales.
To claim a record catch in Wales contact
Mrs Helen Pearce
9 Maes Afallen,
Bow Street, Aberystwyth
SY24 5BL.
Tel 01970 62888 day or 01970 820063 eve.
helen.pearce@btinternet.com

National Federation of Sea Anglers
51A Queen Street,
Newton Abbot
TQ12 2QJ
Tel 01626 331330.
www.nfsa.org.uk
Co-ordinates sea angling clubs and events throughout England (except North West).

Useful Links

www.bbc.co.uk/weather
www.weatheronline.co.uk
www.windfinder.com

Local & Harbour Authorities

Mersey Docks & Harbour Co
Maritime Centre
Seaforth
L21 1LA
Tel 0151 949 6000
Permit Applications:
Tel 0151 949 6144
PORT POLICE
0151 949 1212

SeftonCouncil
Chief Executives Dept
Town Hall, Southport
PR8 1DA
Tel 0845 140 0845

Liverpool City Council
Municipal Buildings
Dale Street
L2 2DH
Tel 0151 233 3000

Wirral Council
Town Hall, Brighton St
Wallasey, Wirral
CH44 8ED
Tel 0151 606 2000

Gwynedd Council
Council Offices
Caernarfon
LL55 1SH
Tel 01286 672255

Anglesey County Council
Council Offices
Llangefni
LL77 7TW
Tel 01248 750057

Conwy C.B.C.
Glan-y-Don, Civic Centre
Colwyn Bay
LL29 8AR
Tel 01492 574000

Denbighshire C.C.
County Hall, Wynnstay Rd,
Ruthin, LL15 1YN
Tel 01824 706000

Flintshire C.C.
County Offices
St David's Park, Ewloe
CH5 3ZQ
Tel 01352 702450

Tidal Information

Laver's Liverpool & Irish Sea Tide Table is the local tidal reference and should be consulted for every trip. The booklets, which run from January to December, are available from August for the following year. There is a diary style format with spaces for notes alongside the tide times and heights. Laver's can also provide monthly tidal information sheets for future years and locations other than Liverpool. Among the 700+ points around the coast are:
Eastham, Hilbre Is., Mostyn Quay, Connah's Quay, Chester, Colwyn Bay, Llandudno, Conwy, Beaumaris, Menai Bridge, Porth Dinorwig, Caernarfon, Fort Belan, Trwyn Dinmor, Moelfre, Amlwch, Cemaes Bay, Holyhead, Trearddur Bay, Porth Trecastell, Llanddwyn Is., Trefor, Porth Dinllaen, Porth Ysgaden, Bardsey Is., Aberdaron, St.Tudwal's Roads, Pwllheli, Criccieth and Porthmadog.
For information about ordering any Laver products go to
www.laverpublishing.com
or contact us at
PO Box 7 Liverpool L19 9EN. Tel 0151 475 7949